Prayer
Oxygen for the Soul

Prayer

Oxygen for the Soul

UNDER THE DIRECTION OF
JACQUES PHILIPPE
AND ANNE OF JESUS (ED.)

 Scepter

This English translation is published by Scepter Publishers, Inc.
info@scepterpublishers.org
www.scepterpublishers.org
800-322-8773
New York

Cover image: Shutterstock.com
Cover design: Marc Whitaker, MTW Design
Page design and composition: Rose Design

Library of Congress Control Number: 2023948921

ISBN paperback: 978-1-59417-519-0
ISBN eBook: 978-1-59417-520-6

Printed in the United States of America

Contents

∞

Introduction
∽

One of the greatest services we can render to people today is to awaken in them the desire for personal prayer, that silent, interior prayer of the heart so recommended by all the saints in the Christian tradition. Every era of spiritual renewal began with a renewal of prayer. It is because men and women sought God with all their heart, to know and love him, and entered into a personal relationship with him, that the Church in certain periods purified herself. The Church rediscovered her fervor, beauty, evangelizing dynamism, and capacity to make herself present to the sufferings of her people.

What renews the Church and saves the world is the living contact with the mystery of God in prayer. That's where we'll find the right answers to the challenges of our time.

It is therefore essential to communicate the thirst for a prayerful encounter with God and to provide the means to persevere faithfully in the practice of interior prayer, despite the inevitable difficulties and struggles. The many ways of meditation offered today reflect a great thirst for inner life. However, for a true encounter with the living God, we need clear and accessible points of reference if meditation is to become a source of inner transformation, of peace, of freer relationships, and of growth in love. We can't be content with a few exercises which, in the end, only lead us to encounter ourselves, without giving us access to the mystery of God.

This book is not a systematic treatise on prayer, but a series of short chapters written by different authors, all members of the Community of the Beatitudes, a contemplative and missionary community comprised of both married and consecrated members. This community "gathers together consecrated sisters and brothers, some of whom are priests; as well as lay members, single and married, including permanent deacons and those who chose to make a vow of lay celibacy."[1] Initially, these texts were intended to encourage and nourish the brothers and sisters of this community in

---

1. "In a Few Words," Community of the Beatitudes, https://beatitudes.org/en/in-a-few-words/.

the life of silent prayer, a fundamental dimension of their vocation.

Each chapter contains a teaching on a particular aspect of the life of interior prayer, which helps us both to see the importance of faithfulness to prayer and to overcome the obstacles on this sometimes difficult path. They also contain quotations from the Church's rich tradition offering practical advice.

May this book help readers put into practice Jesus' invitation in the Gospel *"always to pray and not lose heart"* (Lk 18:1), to experience God's closeness and his presence within us, and to maintain a living contact with the One who is able to renew all things, for he is *"the way, and the truth, and the life"* (Jn 14:6).

1
∽

Why Foster Interior Prayer?

JOUMANA KHALIL

Glory be to Him, Who never felt the need of our praising Him; yet felt the need as being kind to us, and thirsted as loving us, and asks us to give to Him, and longs to give to us.[1]

 St. Ephrem the Syrian

ndeed, why pray? Interior prayer can often be full of pitfalls, poverty, dark nights of the soul, and besides, it takes time. Other forms of prayer such as written and communal prayers and even the Mass, may seem simpler, more accessible, more methodical and adapted to our current schedule.

This call to "friendly intercourse, and frequent solitary converse, with Him Who we know loves

---

1. Ephrem the Syrian, *Hymns on the Nativity*, trans. Philip Schaff, ed. D. P. Curtin (Philadelphia: Dalcassian, 2019), p.15.

us"[2] is one that God often evokes in Scripture, and one to which Jesus never ceases to invite his friends: *"But when you pray, go into your room and shut the door and pray to your Father who is in secret; and your Father who sees in secret will reward you"* (Mt 6:6). Jesus invites us to do this too, he who showed us the importance of it by his own testimony.

Because God is asking me

If God asks me, how can I not trust him? Isn't he my Creator, the One who fashioned me and who alone knows what I need most to complete his creative and sanctifying work in me?

> God, wishing to raise men up to the sharing of the divine life, puts within us the desire to see Him face to face, so that, in this vision, our soul may be consumed by Him who is like a devouring fire, and yearn ever more for union with the Bridegroom: *I have found Him whom my heart loves, I have grasped Him and will not let Him go.*[3]

---

2. Teresa of Ávila, *The Life of Teresa of Jesus: The Autobiography of Teresa of Ávila*, trans. and ed. E. Allison Peers, https://www.carmelite monks.org/Vocation/teresa_life.pdf, p. 62.

3. Community of the Beatitudes, *Book of Life*, no. 57.

If he asks me to pray, it's because he knows what best meets my most vital need: "It is He who makes us desire and who fulfills our desires,"[4] said Thérèse of Lisieux. Yes . . . deep down, it's a question of burning, of desire, of love, of union, of thirst.

Because I'm thirsty for him

In a land that is often dry and sun-scorched, in an arid and silent desert, there is nothing more painful than the physical experience of thirst. The people of the first covenant experienced it all too well. Physical thirst reflects the deepest need of the human soul: the thirst for God.

"My soul thirsts for God, for the living God. When shall I come and behold the face of God?" (Ps 42:2). Many psalms speak of this deep need that dwells in our souls. We are made in God's image but carry this gift of his likeness in clay vessels cracked a thousand times over: *"O God, thou art my God, I seek thee, my soul thirsts for thee; my flesh faints for thee, as in a dry and weary land where no water is"* (Ps 63:1). Jesus knows the human heart, he has visited the deep abyss of its dryness, and he has

---

4. Thérèse of Lisieux to Fr. Adolphe Roulland, November 1, 1896 (Letter 201), Archives of the Carmel of Lisieux, https://archives.carmel delisieux.fr/en/correspondance/lt-201-au-p-roulland-1-novembre-1896/.

come to show us the source of life: *"If anyone is thirsty, let him come to me and drink"* (Jn 7:37).

Thirst drives us to walk and to look for a well or a spring, or to pray for rain. And, in the Bible, the well is the place where love stories are woven. From a spiritual point of view, this walking prompted by thirst pushes our will to enter into spiritual combat. "We believe that the life of prayer enables us to enter into the heart of our beloved, and to find the well deep within ourselves, where we can meet the Beloved, enjoy his beauty and rest in his shadow."[5]

But it's not just our souls that thirst for God. He thirsts for each one of us, too.

Because he thirsts for me

Yes, God thirsts for the love of every human being, and in Jesus he confesses this to us, showing himself in that disarming weakness where our stubborn human reasoning gets trumped. When tired, didn't he ask the Samaritan woman for water, thereby signifying a deeper thirst? And on the Cross, at the height of his work of love, he whispered, as a final word to humanity: *"I thirst"* (Jn 19:28).

---

5. Community of the Beatitudes, *Book of Life,* no. 60.

For this reason, prayerful meditation becomes mutual expectation, shared silence, a dialogue of love: "It is in this way that meditation, pure dialogue of love, takes on an essential place in our lives, for it is the royal road that leads us to the knowledge of the One who is all Love."[6]

If God is love, and love is a gift, he cannot but give of himself. And to give of himself, he must be welcomed. This is his thirst: a thirst for the human heart, the place of his dwelling; of the free acquiescence to his will, a place of poor and humble soil of humanity, so that he may come to inhabit it, purify it, transform it, and irrigate it with his grace. Prayer then becomes the place where the dual desires of man and God come together in a mutual gift.

But this bond created in the Holy Spirit is not closed in on itself. The water poured into the heart of those who pray is also called to become, in turn, a fountain, a spring, an overflow: *"Whoever drinks of the water that I shall give him shall never thirst; the water that I shall give him shall become a spring of water welling up to eternal life"* (Jn 4:14).

---

6. Community of the Beatitudes, *Book of Life*, no. 57.

Because the world is thirsty for God

With Teresa of Ávila, we understand that prayer is also a missionary act. It doesn't stop at the personal experience of divine intimacy, but turns us into apostles who give what we receive, as if by overflowing our cup. We are constantly called to expand the space in our hearts, to embrace the world which is dying of thirst beside a well. If it is true that if we *"look to him . . . so your faces shall never be ashamed"* (Ps 34:5), then what is lived in the secret of our "inner room" cannot but radiate mysteriously around us. The fire, light, living water, and love that the Holy Spirit pours into the heart of a praying soul can only burn, radiate, irrigate, and warm. Through the disconcerting simplicity of this friendly dialogue, the world itself is lifted up toward God.

2

Grace and Struggle

SR. ANNE OF JESUS IDIARTEGARAY

Prayer is to our soul what rain is to the soil. Fertilize the soil ever so richly, it will remain barren unless fed by frequent rains.

St. John Vianney

Prayer—particularly personal interior prayer—is a grace . . . and a struggle, to match. Let us address both of these aspects of prayer with honesty and transparency.

A Grace

Grace means "free gift of God," and is something to be welcomed every day, without any merit on our part. This gift does not depend on us and cannot be taken from us. But for grace to bear fruit, it is up to us to welcome it unceasingly with faith, humility, gratitude, and determination; in a word, with love.

Prayer is not just one grace among many, but one from which all the rest flows, and to which we must constantly return, to immerse all that we are, all that we live, all that we do, and even our most fervent apostolic desires.

Teresa of Ávila says, "Prayer is the door to those great favours which He has bestowed upon me. Once the door is closed, I do not see how He will bestow them."[1]

Drawing from the source, and letting this source nourish our entire existence, is the gift that God never ceases to offer us, and the gift that we can offer him: *"You shall love the Lord your God with all your heart, and with all your soul, and with all your might"* (Dt 6:5).

A battle

The battles we have to wage in order to endure in prayer are not small or insignificant. They are proportionate

---

1. Teresa of Ávila, *Life*, p. 64.

with the gift offered and the stakes involved. Let's take a look at two common temptations.

First temptation

The first temptation we deal with is not setting aside enough time for prayer. Fr. Jacques helps us to overcome this battle by explaining that, for perseverance in prayer,

> we need to set aside certain mistaken feelings of guilt arising from a false notion of charity, and be thoroughly convinced that time given to God is never time stolen from other people who need our love and our presence. On the contrary, fidelity in being present to God guarantees the capacity to be present to others and love them truly. Experience proves this: the love of prayerful souls is the most attentive, delicate, disinterested, sensitive to other people's suffering, and capable of consoling and comforting. Mental prayer makes us better people, and those who are close to us won't complain about that![2]

We must clearly recognize that a life of persevering in prayer bears considerable fruit in our lives. The saints

---

2. Jacques Philippe, *Time for God* (New York: Scepter, 2008), p. 27.

bear witness to this. Our apostolic endeavors will be all the more fruitful if they are rooted in a life of assiduous prayer. As Mother Teresa said, "The more we receive in silent prayer, the more we can give in our active life. We need silence to be able to touch souls."[3]

Second temptation

The second frequent temptation concerns battle of fidelity in friendship and in love, because prayer is a matter of friendship.

> It is not difficult, indeed, to say, "I love you." The difficulty begins when we say "forever," and especially when it comes to realizing it. Because "forever" lasts a long time. [. . .] For, to love the same object forever, you must have a source deep in your soul.
>
> You need both the strength to remember and the strength to create. We must invent every day what must last every day. To love can sometimes be a weakness; but to last in love or friendship is always a generosity, a victory.[4]

3. Mother Teresa, *Total Surrender*, ed. Angelo Devananda Scolozzi (Ann Arbor, MI, Servant, 1985), 107.

4. Père Jérôme, *Œuvres spirituelles* [*Spiritual Works*], vol. 2, *Possibilités et mélodies* (Geneva, Switzerland: Ad Solem, 2011), p. 48.

A decision

Let's not be cowed or discouraged by our difficulties in praying, in being faithful to what we've promised the Lord (or may soon be promising him, if we haven't already!), and let's not lose sight of the beauty of this call.

St. Teresa of Ávila tells us that "prayer cannot be accompanied by self-indulgence,"[5] and she never fails to insist in her writings on the need for "earnest and most determined resolve"[6] in this area. But make no mistake: she is not advocating any idea that we can change the course of events, the effectiveness of our prayer, through our will alone. She simply invites us to place our attention, our loving effort, where it's needed, and to put all our good will into it, whatever the obstacles encountered.

> Another reason [for my account] is to show what great blessings God grants to a soul when He prepares it to love the practice of prayer, though it may not be as well prepared already as it should be; and how, if that soul perseveres, notwithstanding the

---

5. Teresa of Ávila, *The Way of Perfection*, trans. and ed. E. Allison Peers, https://www.carmelitemonks.org/Vocation/Way-of-Perfection.pdf, p. 29.

6. Teresa of Ávila, *The Way of Perfection*, 21, 2. p.72.

sins, temptations and falls of a thousand kinds into
which the devil leads it, the Lord, I am certain, will
bring it to the harbour of salvation, just as, so far as
can at present be told, He has brought me.[7]

So let's keep returning to the heart of the matter:
that of a Love that offers itself to us and desires to be
received. And let us remember that "no feat, no sacri-
fice, accomplished for the beloved but far from him,
will be worthy of the simple loving presence."[8]

Teresa of Ávila also insists that a soul who wishes
to persevere on the path of prayer cannot do so alone.
Aside from the need for spiritual guidance, she speaks
of the benefits of being in contact with other souls of
prayer.[9] Of course, fidelity in the life of prayer is first
and foremost a decision and a personal response to the
question, *"Do you love me?"* (see Jn 21:15–17) posed to
St. Peter, and one that the Lord never ceases to whis-
per to our hearts.

Let these words of Jesus and St. Teresa of Ávila res-
onate in our own hearts:

> *Apart from me, you can do nothing. . . . No longer do I*
> *call you servants, for the servant does not know what his*

---

7. Teresa of Ávila, *Life*, p. 62.

8. Père Jérôme, *Spiritual Works*, vol. 2, p. 46.

9. See Teresa of Ávila, *Life*, p. 60.

master is doing; but I have called you friends, for all that I have heard from my Father I have made known to you. You did not choose me, but I chose you and appointed you that you should go and bear fruit and that your fruit should abide . . . (Jn 15:5; 15–16).

No one who has begun this practice, however many sins he may commit, should ever forsake it. For it is the means by which we may amend our lives again, and without it amendment will be very much harder. So let him not be tempted by the devil, as I was, to give it up for reasons of humility, but let him believe that the words cannot fail of Him Who says that, if we truly repent and determine not to offend Him, He will resume His former friendship with us and grant us the favours which He granted aforetime, and sometimes many more, if our repentance merits it.[10]

---

10. Teresa of Ávila, *Life*, p. 62.

3

Prayer in the Carmelite Tradition

SR. THERESIA SCHUSCHNIGG

[T]he Lord is now pleased to help the gardener, so that He may almost be said to be the gardener Himself, for it is He Who does everything.[1]

ST. TERESA OF ÁVILA

Watering our garden

The great masters of Carmelite prayer, St. John of the Cross and St. Teresa of Ávila, use images to describe the path of prayer.[2] Here we take up another symbol used by Teresa of Ávila. She describes the life of prayer with the image of a garden that we must

---

1. Teresa of Ávila *Life*, p. 95.

2. See *The Ascent of Mount Carmel*, and *Interior Castle*.

water.[3] This garden is our soul. The gardener is God. He clears the undergrowth and sows beautiful plants. Then he entrusts us with their care. Our task is not to plant or uproot, but to water. Plants represent virtues. The water represents the graces received in prayer.[4]

Teresa describes four ways of watering this garden, corresponding to the different stages of the life of prayer. The Master of Creation hands over his work to us with great love and trust, and calls us to collaborate with him: a relationship of friendship and trust in which the primary initiative is always that of the Master, but in which, without the response of the disciple, the work will not be completed, the work cannot fully unfold. Water is always given, albeit in different ways, but it is not used for its own sake, nor for the gardener's enjoyment; it is used for the plants. The graces of prayer serve to increase our capacity to love.

Let's take a brief look at these four ways of watering.

---

3. See Teresa of Ávila, *Life*, chaps. 11 and 14, among others.

4. In interpreting this passage, we rely primarily on Thomas H. Green SJ, *When the Well Runs Dry: Prayer Beyond the Beginnings* (Notre Dame, IN: Ave Maria Press, 2007), p. 30 ff.

The well

With the help of a bucket, we pull water from the well. It's slow, tiring, and inefficient: a lot of work for little water. But it allows our plants to grow. In prayer, this corresponds to one stage of mental prayer: reflection on our life, on our daily experiences, in the light of the Gospel. Taking an honest look at ourselves, realizing what we've done and what we're doing, is not always easy.

We've all experienced it: we long for silence and contemplation, but as soon as there's an opportunity to enter, we back away. Here, only a firm resolve not to turn back can help.

The noria

The same methods and prayer themes give us access to water much more quickly. Teresa uses the image of the noria, a hydraulic wheel and bucket device that scoops water out of the well much more easily. Suddenly, the Lord multiplies the results of our efforts. Everything comes to life, everything begins to speak to us of his love. Up to now, we've struggled to know the Lord and to know ourselves. Now, this knowledge opens us to the joy of encounter. This is what Teresa calls recollected prayer.

The river

There's nothing to do but direct this living water to the plants. It's from this stage onward that we speak of supernatural graces. Prayer is always a gift. But in the first two stages, our active part is more important. The experience of meditative prayer puts us in a position to welcome what only God can give: the graces of passive prayer.

The rain

The most efficient way to water our garden is the gentle but abundant rain of spring. We have nothing left to do but sit back and welcome grace, allowing it to penetrate us.

In these last two steps, we simply give God our time and our person to act as he wills. We are the clay in the hands of the potter. It sounds easy, but in the end it's the hardest thing for us. It's a matter of complete surrender to let go of all control, "to stop swimming and turn onto our backs to float and let the water take us where it will."[5]

---

5. Green, p. 142.

Drought

Let's mention one more phenomenon: dryness. It exists at all these stages. But once we've verified that it's not due to our laziness or unfaithfulness, we can embrace it as another way of being united with Christ. This topic will be delved into in another chapter, but it must be said that it seems like we need to go through these times of trial in order to learn to truly love. The amazing thing throughout it all is that, despite the drought, our garden does not completely dry out.

An art of living

How does this apply to our life? We pray, we meditate . . . but perhaps we can start by considering the following points:

- Every good thing, every exchange in prayer, comes from a loving relationship between the Creator and his creature
- The initiative is always God's
- Our personal responsibility to collaborate with him remains imperative
- The practice of human virtue enables a greater response to grace, frequent use of the sacraments

of Holy Eucharist and Penance, mortification, atonement, and the intercession of the saints

- Prayer is a dynamic process directed by the Holy Spirit, where in silence and inner vigilance, we recognize his movements
- Adapting to his process with trust and abandon leads to fruitfulness
- The goal is union with the Beloved
- This union overflows into union with everything created

Our lives gradually become centered on God, so that relationships—with him, with ourselves, with our loved ones, with the world—are at the heart of our existence. Formed by the life of prayer in all these relationships, we collaborate in the work of the gardener. We are the branch connected to Christ, who is the vine. The fruit is his business. We have only one thing to do: fix our gaze and attention on the Vine and draw its sap.

4

An Act of Faith

FR. JACQUES PHILIPPE

Mary will share her faith with you. . . . It will cause you to depend less upon sensible and extraordinary feelings. For it is a lively faith animated by love enabling you to do everything from no other motive than that of pure love. It is a firm faith, unshakable as a rock, prompting you to remain firm and steadfast in the midst of storms and tempests.[1]

ST. LOUIS-MARIE GRIGNION DE MONTFORT

I n the prologue to *The Ascent of Mount Carmel*, St. John of the Cross writes: "There are many souls who think they have no prayer and yet have much, and others, on the contrary, who think they have much and have

---

1. Louis-Marie Grignion de Montfort, *True Devotion to the Blessed Virgin*, chap. 6, no. 2, www.catholictreasury.info/books/true_devotion/td27.php#bk1.

very little." In other words, some think they pray well but actually pray badly, while others feel they pray badly because their prayer feels poor, but in fact pray very well!

This observation forces us to ask ourselves: What makes prayer good—bringing us closer to God, transforming us little by little—or superficial? The answer is simple: for our prayer to be good, it must be an act of faith, an act of hope, and an act of love. These three theological virtues are the essential dynamism of the spiritual life, and therefore also of prayer. These virtues unite us to God.

In practice, we can pray in many different ways: meditating on Scripture, pouring out our hearts before God, remaining in adoring silence, reciting the rosary or using the Jesus Prayer[2] . . . all methods are good, as long as the fundamental disposition of the heart is an attitude of faith, hope, and love. In this chapter, we'll focus on faith.

As soon as a person starts praying, they are implicitly making an act of faith: "I believe that God exists, that he loves me, that it's worth spending time with him." This act of faith, often imperfect, not always accompanied by intense feelings or great enlightenment, is nonetheless essential.

---

2. For more on the Jesus Prayer, see chapter 8.

Faith is the gateway to the mystical life. It's what brings us into real contact with God. "The greater is the faith of the soul, the more closely is it united with God,"[3] says St. John of the Cross. Union with God is not measured by the intensity of the emotions we feel, or the abundance of light that illuminates our intelligence, but by the sincerity of our act of faith. Of course, the human faculties play an important role in the life of prayer, especially sensitivity and intelligence, but we need to situate them carefully.

The role and limits of sensitivity

When sensibility is touched, when the heart feels beautiful emotions in prayer, it's good. This encourages and enlivens our faith, making us experience that God is not an abstract notion but a living reality capable of touching our hearts deeply.

However, emotional feelings cannot be the foundation of our prayer life. We can "taste" God, but all we can taste of God is not yet God. He is infinitely greater than anything human sensibility can grasp.

---

3. John of the Cross, *The Ascent of Mount Carmel*, 3rd rev. ed., trans. and ed. E. Allison Peers, www.catholicspiritualdirection.org/ascent carmel.pdf, p. 108.

So we mustn't get too attached to it. We run the risk of becoming more interested in God's gifts, than in God himself. We could also worry, thinking ourselves far from God, or feeling guilty for praying badly when we no longer feel anything in prayer. When we experience such aridity we shouldn't worry, but welcome it as an invitation to practice faith in a purer way and remember that what really puts us in touch with God is not the intensity of emotions but the determination of faith.

Faith sets us free—free to welcome with gratitude the feelings of joy and love that God sometimes graces us with, but also free to persevere in aridity without troubling us. Faith is enough; it lets us touch God and allows God to touch us and work secretly in our hearts. We may not realize it at the time, but one day we'll see the fruits.

Role and limits of intelligence

We can make a similar point about the intelligence. When the intellect receives enlightenment on the richness of the mysteries of faith, this is of course a grace. We must also strive as far as possible to understand what we believe, to develop our understanding of the realities of faith. As for our concrete life, when we receive enlightenment on our personal journey, on the decisions we need to make, this is also very precious. But then again, the truth of prayer cannot be measured by the amount of light that illuminates our intelligence. God sometimes allows times of darkness, which are normal. What we understand about God is not yet God. Some truths of faith are beyond our understanding. What's more, God doesn't answer all our questions, and doesn't always give us the lights we'd like to have.

These moments when our intelligence is in the dark can be painful, but they are necessary. They prevent us from falling into the temptation of reducing God to the measure of our intelligence. They also purify us from what can sometimes be a distorted exercise of intelligence.

In the use of our intellectual faculties, there can be a pride in knowledge, a curiosity or a search for human security, in which we say to ourselves, "I've got it all figured out, so I'm in the clear!" Sometimes, too, there is a stubbornness to hold power, in which we think, "knowledge is mastery." Our intelligence needs to learn humility, to recognize its limits, to let go of any pretension to control and dominate.

That's why God sometimes places us in the dark. But then faith comes to our rescue: "I don't understand, but that doesn't prevent me from believing, hoping, and loving." St. John of the Cross speaks of faith by which we love God without a clear comprehension of him.[4]

Here again, faith sets us free: free to joyfully welcome the light God gives us, but also free to walk in darkness, abandoning ourselves to God.

It is therefore very consoling to understand how faith is the true foundation of prayer, which truly puts us in contact with God, unites us with him and enables him to act in us. The aridities and obscurities encountered in the life of prayer are painful, but they enable us to become adults in the faith.

This path of faith is not intended to devalue or destroy our human faculties, sensibility, and intelligence, but to purify them and make them fit to reach the One who is their ultimate object.

Paradoxically, accepting dryness and obscurity in prayer will make our sensitivity finer, more capable of tasting God, and will also make our intelligence more penetrating to contemplate the grandeur of his mysteries. Let us ask for this grace of steadfastness in faith, and invoke the Virgin Mary to give us a share in her faith.

---

4. John of the Cross, *A Spiritual Canticle of the Soul and the Bridegroom Christ*, trans. David Lewis, rev. Harry Plantinga (digital ed., 1995), prologue, no. 4, pp. 7–8. www.documentacatholicaomnia.eu.

5

An Act of Hope

FR. JACQUES PHILIPPE

With respect to God, the more the soul hopes, the more it attains [union with God].[1]

ST. JOHN OF THE CROSS

For our prayer to be true, to bring us into contact with God and gradually transform us, it must be an act of faith, an act of hope, an act of love. Let's now look at prayer as an act of hope.

Prayer is an act of hope because when we start praying we're counting on God, expecting everything we need from him.

This attitude of hope is particularly important because there can be no life of prayer without a certain experience of poverty, which can sometimes be

---

1. John of the Cross, *The Ascent of Mount Carmel*, 3rd rev. ed., trans. and ed. E. Allison Peers (Garden City, NJ: Image, 1962; digital ed., 1994), p. 198, www.catholicspiritualdirection.org/ascentcarmel.pdf.

very painful. Prayer is a paradoxical reality: at times it makes us feel immense happiness, a fullness greater than anything the world can offer, but at other times, great poverty.

Why is this inevitable?

Poor in front of God

First of all, the inevitability exists because there's no technique that will enable us to always pray well.

God is the Master; we depend on him, he who sometimes remains silent and hidden despite our efforts, and who sometimes visits us and fulfills us without our having deserved it. We cannot plan or program divine grace and blessings!

On the other hand, prayer leads us deeper and deeper into God's light, sometimes joyful and consoling, but sometimes painful and humiliating, as it brings our imperfections, our sins, our wounds into clear focus. Just as a ray of sunlight shines through a dark room, revealing the smallest speck of dust suspended in the air, so God's light inexorably highlights our misery.

It is in the solitude and silence of prayer, away from our usual supports, that all our downfalls and mistakes, our difficulty in recollecting ourselves, our remorse for the past, our fears for the future, our anger and bitterness, our pride and hardness of heart, are brought to the surface. It is much more comfortable to immerse ourselves into work, browse the internet, or chat with friends! The experience of poverty is so difficult that our desire for holiness must be stronger.

What often makes us shy away from silent prayer is fear, because we sense that, inexorably, if we stand in God's presence, he will attack our mediocrity and bring to light everything in our lives that needs to be purified.

This experience of poverty should not, however, worry us; it is normal and even absolutely necessary.

Of course, prayer is not the only experience of poverty. It's the whole of life and its difficult situations, that sometimes make us feel our frailties, our wounds, our sins. But prayer intensifies our awareness of all this, and forces us to confront it without any possible way out.

Practice hope

It is then that prayer must become an act of hope, which can be expressed as follows: "I remember that *'Those who are well have no need of a physician, but those who are sick'* (Mt 9:12) and *'I came not to call the righteous, but sinners'* (Mk 2:17). I put all my hope in you! I hope and expect everything from you, from your goodness and mercy! I rely on you alone, not on myself!"

What saves us from sadness and discouragement is a dual attitude: humility and hope. It's a matter of fully accepting what we are, accepting the cruel revelation of our limitations and faults, but using them to learn to put all our trust and hope in God alone, rather than in our abilities and achievements.

"For everyone who exalts himself will be humbled, but he who humbles himself will be exalted" (Lk 18:14). With these words, the Gospel invites us to recognize and fully accept our misery, however deep and painful it may be, and to throw ourselves into God's arms, with blind trust in his mercy and power.

We must accept that we are radically poor, and transform this poverty into a cry, an expectation, an invincible hope, even if it means hoping against hope! (see Rom 4:18). God will then come to our rescue.

This poor man cried, and the Lord heard him, and saved him out of all his troubles (Ps 34:6).

For he has not despised or abhorred the affliction of the afflicted; and he has not hid his face from him, but has heard, when cried to him (Ps 22:24).

The prayer that God hears is that of the poor: *"The prayer of the humble pierces the clouds"* (Sir 35:17).

Unwelcome is the Pharisee, who is satisfied with himself and his good deeds and despises others; but the Publican, who stands at a distance and beats his breast, says: *"God, be merciful to me a sinner!"* (Lk 18:13).

The prayer that touches God's heart and draws his grace is the one that springs from the depths of our misery and sin. *"Out of the depths I cry to thee, O Lord! Lord, hear my voice!"* (Ps 130:1–2).

Fidelity to prayer is a school of humility and hope. It is by accepting our poverty and our nakedness before God, and expecting everything from his mercy, that we will gradually receive healing, purification, consolation and peace.

In the words of St. Thérèse of Lisieux:

> So let's stay far away from everything that shines, love our littleness, love to feel nothing, then we will be poor in spirit and Jesus will come to get us, however far we are he will transform us into flames of love.[2]

---

2. Thérèse of Lisieux to Sister Marie of the Sacred Heart, September 17, 1896 (Letter 197) https:// archives.carmeldelisieux.fr/en/ correspondance/lt-197-a-soeur-marie-du-sacre-coeur-17-septembre-1896/.

6

Prayer and Receptivity

SR. THERESIA SCHUSCHNIGG

Too easily we think of holiness as something we acquire. We do not acquire it but we must labour to prepare for God's coming to us and work with him when he draws near.[1]

RUTH BURROWS

Have you ever heard that, in prayer, the essential thing is to be receptive, to put aside our frenetic daily activity in order to receive? And did you feel a vague frustration at the time, thinking, "Easy to say, but how can I do it?"

What do we mean by a receptive attitude in prayer? Why is it so important? How can we grow in this sense?

---

1. Ruth Burrows, *To Believe in Jesus* (Mahwah, NJ: HiddenSpring, 2010), p. 89.

Some anthropological aspects

At creation, "*God formed man of dust from the ground, and breathed into his nostrils the breath of life; and man became a living being*" (Gn 2:7). Since then, breathing has been the sure sign of life. We breathe without having to think about it, in a rhythm of our own that inhabits us and "works" on its own. If God were to stop giving us the breath of life, we'd cease to exist right now. We are creatures who receive every moment of our lives from the loving will of our Creator.

Let's take a second fundamental aspect of our created being: "*Then the Lord God said, 'It is not good that the man should be alone'*" (Gn 2:18). He gave him a helper, a companion like himself.

We are created as relational beings, radically dependent on others. We are all born of others, and become adults through the gift of others. The adult human being becomes autonomous and capable of giving life in his turn—which again presupposes that he lives in relationship. No one can live self-sufficiently, and the capacity for autonomy can become a trap. We are free to cut ourselves off from others, to become self-sufficient, to root ourselves in activism, control, and misunderstood responsibility. It may then become necessary to relearn the attitude of receptivity.

How often do we feel stuck or dissatisfied with the quality of our human relationships, simply because we think we know everything about the other person, and no longer make the effort to welcome him or her as a constantly renewed gift?

The same is true of our relationship with God, all the more so because in our relationship with him we depend most obviously on his initiative. If he didn't reveal himself, if he didn't give of himself, we'd have no way of knowing him or entering into a relationship with him. He loves us first!

Receptivity

Let's be careful not to misunderstand the passive aspect of this attitude. There are different stages and periods in the life of prayer. The deepening of our prayer life is generally accompanied by a simplification of methods and a more passive presence on the part of the praying person. But it doesn't matter where we are in our journey: receptivity is key. To truly enter into this "great blessing" with God of which Teresa of Ávila speaks,[2] we must reach out with all our being to the

---

2. See Teresa of Ávila, *Life*, p. 62.

one who loves us. This is as true for those who practice vocal or mental prayer as it is for those who pray in the silence of simple loving presence. It is the Spirit who leads in the life of prayer.

For our part, we can make ourselves available to his action by cultivating receptivity, the attitude of empty hands and spiritual childhood. It's not so easy for people who are so used to seeking independence, power, and possession, to allow others to surprise us, but also to approach them without preconceptions, without knowing everything, without goals or plans. Let's face it, it costs us, this way of letting go. But we must stop trying to control everything, and open up to the unknown. Jesus warned us: *"Apart from me you can do nothing"* (Jn 15:5). He says this not to show us our powerlessness, but to call us to him, so that we allow him to give us everything we need.

How to progress

Receptivity is inscribed deep within us. So it's simply a matter of reconnecting with what we've left behind.

Our bodies offer us some precious help in this matter. We can start by paying attention to our breathing or the beating of our hearts, perceiving the life that inhabits us, offered to us, by he who gives us life. Many meditation techniques recommend this simple attention to the rhythm of breathing. It is indeed an anchor to establish ourselves in our state as creatures, a state which is received from the Creator at every moment.

Certain prayer gestures can also help: opening our hands to express that we are not holding anything back, that we are moving toward the Other to put ourselves at his service. The way we sit or kneel can express openness, interest, respect, listening, and the desire to receive.

Also, no matter the manner of prayer at the moment, we must ask ourselves: "Where is my focus? Am I focused primarily on myself, my worries and joys, my plans and desires?" The "problem" with God is that he's very polite and delicate. Where a neighbor would have interrupted long ago in our interminable discourses on self, the Lord will listen with unflappable patience. He is an expert in receptivity. We must continue this inner dialogue and ask ourselves: "What if I dared to trust God, who knows me better than I know myself, and doesn't need long explanations to understand what's in my heart? What if I took a little interest in what's in his Heart?"

So what's going on?

Most of the time, the exchange in prayer is not a big deal, or rather, it's very big, but unnoticed: we put ourselves in the presence of our God, offering him time and space: let him do as he will!

May he continue in each of us his work as Creator and Redeemer. It may be that we taste something of his action; often this is not the case. Whatever the case, he acts on our psyche, will, intelligence, and senses—in short, on our entire being, transforming it little by little and making it more and more alive and like himself.

Receptivity opens us up to what God alone can do in us and for us. We will see the fruits of this in our everyday lives when we become capable of receiving reality with gratitude and respect, as it is given to us.

7

∾

Meditation and Contemplation

FR. JACQUES PHILIPPE

It is not so essential to think much as to love much.[1]

ST. TERESA OF ÁVILA

Methodical prayer

The transition from meditation to contemplation is an important theme in the work of John of the Cross. He writes about it in three of his works, *The Ascent of Mount Carmel*, *The Dark Night*, and *The Living Flame of Love*.

During his era, many people (both lay and religious) under a variety of influences, developed the

---

1. Teresa of Ávila, *The Interior Castle*, trans. Benedictines of Stanbrook, rev. Benedict Zimmerman, OCD, 3rd ed. (London: Thomas Baker, 1921), p. 93, http://www.ccel.org/ccel/teresa/castle2.html.

practice of silent prayer. The practice required a certain method to be followed, involving, for example, the following elements: devoting half an hour or an hour of one's time to it every day, begin with an interior preparation and an invocation to recollect oneself and place oneself in the presence of God; reading a text from Scripture or a spiritual author; imagining and reflecting on the text to draw from it inspiration for the intelligence; drawing up feelings to excite the heart in the love of God; making concrete resolutions for application in life. A prayer follows, entrusting these resolutions to God and asking him for the strength to put them into practice, concluding with thanksgiving.

Countless books offered such methods to the faithful who wished to progress in their spiritual life and union with God. In those days, for fear of spiritual delusion, it was frowned upon for anyone to practice silent prayer without having a book with them, and without relying on such a method.

John of the Cross did not reject these methods; indeed, he saw how they could be very useful, even necessary, to help someone engage in and persevere on the path of prayer. They show us how to proceed concretely in prayer, and how to avoid the inner emptiness and laziness that can sometimes threaten us. They train the soul to frequent God, to detach from the things of the world, and to be open to the enlightenment and graces that the Lord can bestow. Even today, similar methods, adapted to a modern way of thinking—it's a good idea, for example, to involve the body—can be invaluable for entering into the life of prayer.

Limits of these methods

John of the Cross insisted, however, that although these methods are good, they have their limitations. They are based above all on human activity (of the intellect, the imagination, and the will), whereas prayer is destined to become gradually less "active" and more "passive," not so much an activity of humans as an attitude of receptivity, where it is God who operates in the soul.

On the other hand, he points out that, while the emotions, thoughts, and resolutions we experience in prayer can bring us closer to God, they are insufficient to unite us with him and allow us to be deeply transformed. What we feel about God is not yet God. What we understand about God is not yet God. What we imagine of God is not yet God. He is beyond all representations and impressions.

Another limitation of these methods is as follows: experience shows that, for a time, they can "work well" (we receive enlightenment, our hearts warm up in love, we get a real taste of God's presence, it feels good and encourages us to persevere), but there generally comes a time when this exercise doesn't "work" any more. We enter a drought and no longer feel any desire for it; it becomes laborious and tedious. We become reluctant to meditate and instead are compelled to stop talking and thinking, and to be still in simple, loving attention to God's presence, without words, ideas, or distinct images.

Drought, an entrance into contemplation?

This phenomenon of dryness[2] and powerlessness or inability to meditate is disconcerting for those who are used to meditating and find it satisfying. But it is generally a good sign: the Lord wants to give the person the grace of a poorer, simpler, more receptive prayer, which will ultimately be the source of great progress, for it is now God who is at work. In a secret, imperceptible but real way, he will act in the depths of the heart, infusing wisdom and strength that will enable the person to go much further.

---

2. On the subject of dryness, see also chapter 13.

Drought is not necessarily a sign of this new stage. John of the Cross gives criteria for discernment. In addition to the inability to meditate, two other signs are needed. Firstly, that the person has no desire to distract himself with anything other than God. Secondly, that he or she feels a kind of inner inclination where

> the soul takes pleasure in being alone, and waits with loving attentiveness upon God, without making any particular meditation, in inward peace and quietness and rest, and without acts and exercises of the faculties—memory, understanding and will—at least, without discursive acts, that is, without passing from one thing to another; the soul is alone, with an attentiveness and a knowledge, general and loving, as we said, but without any particular understanding, and adverting not to that which it is contemplating.[3]

Contemplation

This is what John of the Cross calls contemplation. A simple, poor prayer, more receptive than active; a loving attention of the heart to the presence of God. This loving attention can coexist with certain involuntary

---

3. John of the Cross, *Ascent of Mount Carmel*, p. 119.

distractions of the imagination and thoughts which cannot be totally stopped except by very special grace. Thoughts may wander a little, but the heart is turned towards God in a simple act of faith and love, and that's enough!

Sometimes this contemplation has a specific purpose: we are touched by a particular aspect of God's mystery. We may marvel at the beauty of Jesus' face, or at the power of one of his words.

But it can also happen that this contemplation has no precise object, that it is like a general and obscure view of the mystery of God, a mystery of love beyond all conception, an elusive but living presence welcomed in faith and gratitude. This is all very well, for God is at work here, secretly communicating himself to the soul. The fruits will come in abundance. The soul is strengthened in faith, hope, and charity.

The transition to contemplation is not a definitive end to other types of prayer. When the grace of a prayer of simple loving attention is not given, or when circumstances require us to meditate on a text or a truth, it is good to return to meditation. Nor should we forget that, whatever our spiritual stage, moments of meditation on Scripture are always indispensable.

8

Heartfelt Prayer

FR. ISAAC AUDHUY

The prayer of the heart is simply a means to find the way which will lead me into this attitude with regard to the Father, by which he hallows his name in me.[1]

DOM ANDRÉ POISSON

P rayer of the Heart, or "continual prayer," has its origins in St. Paul's invitation to the Christians of Thessalonica: *"Pray constantly"* (1 Thes 5:17). Often, when we think of prayer of the heart, we think of the prayer of monks and the Jesus Prayer.

One may also think of the story *The Way of a Pilgrim*, the 19th century Russian story of a peasant who renounces the world to wander and pray the Prayer of

---

1. A Carthusian [Dom André Poisson], *Letter to a Friend on the Prayer of the Heart*, trans. a Cistercian (orig. French, 2001), https://coramfratribus.com/wp-content/uploads/2022/03/A-Carthusian-Prayer-of-the-Heart-1.pdf.

the Heart, or the Jesus Prayer, obeying Christ's invitation to pray unceasingly. Many Christians in the West have discovered with wonder the Orthodox tradition: icons, Byzantine liturgy, some famous Orthodox saints like St. Seraphim of Sarov, and the collection of traditional texts on Orthodox prayer, the *Philokalia.*

The prayer of the Holy Spirit in our hearts

Prayer of the Heart is also called continual prayer or the Jesus Prayer, for it is Jesus who is invoked in this short invocation: "Lord Jesus, Son of God, have mercy on me, a sinner," often set to the rhythm of our breathing. We should recognize, however, that Prayer of the Heart is not identified with a single formula. Continual prayer can be based on the traditional formula mentioned above, or can also focus on a single word, such as "Jesus" or "Abba." Some may even use the word *Ruah* (Spirit)—which acts as an inner Epiclesis, calling the Spirit into our hearts—or the invocation "Jesus, Mary, Joseph."

The method, a path to union with God

A method, however inspired, is never an end in itself. It is one path among others, the goal being to lead to union with God.

As well as this search of and this action of God, its aim is also to control thoughts. In other words, how can we simplify and channel this perpetual inner agitation and redirect it towards God? A short invocation, recited alone, can therefore be a support and a shield against the interference of bubbling inner thoughts.

Each word in these formulas have their own importance, to enter gradually into this divine communion, and make us captive to it. We can understand that, for many saints who were "animated by the Breath," prayer had become as natural as breathing, in all aspects of their lives, in the humblest activities of their lives, as well as in their sleep. As the Song of Solomon says: *"I slept, but my heart was awake"* (Song 5:2).

Philokalia, the call to beauty

The Greek word *philokalia* means the love of the beautiful. Spiritual beauty is that of God, which he desires to chisel into our hearts through his Holy Spirit. It is also the beauty of baptismal grace, which grows in its full vocation. We are made for divine beauty, for God is infinitely beautiful. How can God, through the Holy Spirit, not work at chiseling our hearts into something beautiful, since we have been made *theophores*, God-bearers?

Continual prayer not only has an educational or technical aspect in the fight against thoughts, it is above all a profession of theological and even Trinitarian faith.

Such is the case with the formula, "Lord Jesus, Son of God, have mercy on me, a sinner." According to one explanation of the Fathers: "Lord" refers to the Holy Spirit, without whom we cannot say *"Jesus is Lord"* (see 1 Cor 12:3); "Jesus" refers to the Savior; "Son of God" is linked to the Father.

The plea *"God, be merciful to me a sinner!"* is that of the publican justified by the Lord in Luke's Gospel (Lk 18:13).

Everyone's prayer is made up of regularity and fidelity, through trials and effort. Indeed, the time for growth comes through humble, patient practice.

God within us

Yes, prayer is hard work, it's not magic! It is the work of God within us, with the contribution of our *"two pennies"* (see Mk 12:42). The rosary is, one might say, the "prayer-weaving shuttle."

The repetition of the name of Jesus or of the short Prayer of the Heart gathers our hearts, closes the door to distractions, and introduces us to his presence.

May the Holy Spirit lead our hearts towards ever-simpler and deeper prayer.

9

How to Spend Your Prayer Time

FR. JACQUES PHILIPPE

In our ordinary lives, we share our abilities with the world. In our prayer, we offer our share of powerlessness. This is what makes our prayer possible and relevant. Nothing should prohibit it, not even our inability to pray.[1]

MARTIN STEFFENS

The time devoted to prayer is very precious. You need to have a strong desire to make the most of it, so that it is fruitful rather than routine. It is, nevertheless, an area of great personal freedom: each person must discover how the Holy Spirit gradually shapes his or her dialogue with God. Without

---

1. Martin Steffens, "Prayer," *La Croix*, April 17, 2020.

wishing to impose any rules or set any limits, let's say a few words on the subject.

When the question doesn't arise

Sometimes the question of how the Holy Spirit is moving our hearts doesn't even arise: we easily enter a state of recollection, a loving attention to God that is enough for us. Or our hearts spontaneously pour out before the Lord. Or we receive the particular grace of a strong influence of God where we let him become the total master of our prayer. Or, in the midst of a difficult trial, our prayer becomes an instinctual cry to God from the depths of our misery. At other times, however, the question arises of how the Holy Spirit wants our hearts to move: we're not spontaneously drawn to this or that way of praying, and it's up to us to decide how to spend this time.

The beginning and the end

First, we need to pay attention to how we begin this prayer time by settling into the present moment, by putting ourselves truly in the presence of God, in an act of love and faith, in a great desire to take advantage of this immense gift we have been given, that of having a an encounter with the Lord. We can invoke the

Holy Spirit, entrust ourselves to Mary, or enter into this very special moment in some other way.

As to the end: even if we don't consider the time spent in prayer to have been of the highest quality, we should never leave sad or discouraged. Spending time with God is always a gift, and we should thank him warmly for it.

Even if we weren't very present, he was, and certainly did something in our hearts! We must always leave in gratitude, certain that we can count on the Lord. A prayer that has "failed" for most of the time can be "salvaged" in the last three minutes by a great act of humility and trust, and a strong resolve to continue on its way with God. Gratitude should be even greater if we have experienced a beautiful moment; and the resolve stronger to move forward, if we have received enlightenment from God.

The in-between

What can we say about this "in-between" period of prayer?

There are, of course, innumerable ways of spending time with the Lord: talking to him spontaneously, thanking him, invoking his grace, presenting him with our needs and those of the world. We can ruminate on a text from Scripture, repeating it and letting it penetrate our hearts, considering it in all that it says to us. . . . We can lean on a psalm that we love and that does us good. We can also (especially if we're very distracted and find it hard to collect ourselves) read a few lines from a spiritual work that speaks to us and puts us back in tune with God, in listening, and in nourishing our good dispositions of trust, love, and generosity.

The Prayer of the Heart can also be a great help: simply and softly repeating the name of Jesus, while being attentive to his presence in our hearts.

Another possibility, and not the least important, is the recitation of the Rosary. Especially in difficult times, the Rosary can be the prayer of those who can no longer pray; in this humble, simple way, Mary can share with us her recollection and openness to God.

Of course, the various occupations described above can be combined in the same period of prayer. But it is important to avoid "flitting about," and to strive for a certain continuity in a form of prayer during the same period of prayer.

The rule in this area is simple: let's do what does us good, what helps us to be attentive to God's presence, to welcome his love, which nourishes our faith, our hope, our charity.

Sometimes the only thing left to do is to confide in God our powerlessness to pray! Standing there, despite dryness, boredom, and even disgust, can be a genuine prayer—all the more so as there's no self-gratification involved!

Active or passive prayer

A key question is that of discerning when to be active and when to be passive in prayer.

Sometimes we have to be active, otherwise nothing happens—we get lazy and stuck in a rut. We need to meditate, read, talk, get moving and actively nourish our faith, our hope, and our love.

Sometimes, on the contrary, we need to put aside reading, meditation, and activity, and instead remain still and silent, because the Holy Spirit gives us the gift of entering into a contemplative grace: we feel an inclination in our heart to remain peaceful, without any particular activity of the intellect, but in a simple loving attention to the presence of God.

Thought and imagination can go here and there, but in the heart there is a loving attention to God, and that's enough. There's no need for a lot of thoughts and words, but simply to maintain this loving attention of the heart.

Full of God's riches

If we are faithful to prayer and do our best to make good use of it, with God's grace, we will one day be able to say, like the soul spoken of by St. John of the Cross in his *Spiritual Canticle*: "[The soul] has nothing of the world to hope for, and nothing spiritual to desire, seeing that it feels itself to be full of the riches of God."[2]

May the Holy Spirit bless our good will and give us the necessary fidelity and discernment.

---

2. John of the Cross, *Spiritual Canticle*, stanzas 20–21, no. 12, p. 91.

10

Prayer or Worship?

FR. JACQUES PHILIPPE

Worship . . . is the perception of the greatness, the majesty, and the beauty of God together with his goodness and his presence that take our breath away. It is a kind of sinking into the bottomless and unbounded ocean of the majesty of God. To worship, according to the saying of St. Angela of Foligno, is "to recollect oneself in unity and [plunge] our whole soul in the divine infinity."[1]

RANIERO CANTALAMESSA

When teaching about prayer, we often ask: what's the difference between prayer and worship? They are two distinct realities, but they can also coincide. Prayer is something broader. To

---

1. Raniero Cantalamessa, Fourth Lenten Homily, April 4, 2019, https://www.ewtn.com/catholicism/library/fourth-lenten-homily-2019-3242.

revisit Teresa of Ávila's famous expression: "Mental prayer, in my view, is nothing but friendly intercourse, and frequent solitary converse, with Him Who we know loves us."[2] It is a personal, silent form of prayer in which we express and deepen our intimate relationship with God. It can be experienced in many settings (although aided by those that allow for silence and recollection). It involves a variety of inner acts and attitudes: pouring out one's heart to God, supplication, thanksgiving, listening, meditation, contemplation, and so on.

Worship, on the other hand, is the most fundamental human relationship with God, whether in silent prayer or in other forms of personal or community prayer. The starting point is a gesture: that of genuflection, of prostration, as a sign of respect and submission. *"O come, let us worship and bow down, let us kneel before the Lord, our Maker! For he is our God, and we are the people of his pasture, and the sheep of his hand"* (Ps 95:6–7).

In its religious sense, worship can only be addressed to God, the one and living God, as the whole of Scripture forcefully proclaims. *"You shall fear the Lord your God"* (Dt 10:20). *"You shall worship the Lord your God,*

---

2. Teresa of Ávila, *Life*, chapter p. 62.

and him only shall you serve" (Lk 4:8). Woe be to the one who worships anything other than God, for in the end he will find death and ruin. Happy, on the contrary, is the one who knows how to kneel before God, who will be able to stand upright and face all the storms of life.

This gesture of worship must, of course, express an inner attitude, already present in the Old Testament, and evoked by Jesus in his dialogue with the Samaritan woman as a grace of the new times, a gift of the Spirit:

> But the hour is coming, and now is, when the true worshipers will worship the Father in spirit and truth, for such the Father seeks to worship him. God is spirit, and those who worship him must worship in spirit and truth. (Jn 4:23–24)

Worship is the attitude of man who perceives his fragility and smallness, and at the same time the immensity and infinite greatness of God. It's a paradoxical attitude, made up of both happiness and fear. It's as if man is confounded, reduced to nothing by the perception of divine greatness, but at the same time he's overjoyed to find himself face to face with "something" that infinitely surpasses him, and whose beauty and majesty fascinates him. He finds deep joy in having "something" to admire and love that surpasses all understanding and surpasses all beauty. This "something" is freely given to him, and that is far more vast and splendid than the work of his hands.

Gestures of worship

The primary gesture of worship is prostration, but there are also other gestures to express it, such as the praise of the lips, which feel compelled to reveal that which dwells in the heart. It's interesting to note that, for Scripture, "pure lips" are those that invoke and praise the Lord, while those that address idols are impure.

The deeper the worship, the more the words simplify, becoming a brief "Praise be to you" or "My Lord and my God," or a simple acquiescence: "Amen!" "To worship is in fact to consent. It is letting God be God," says Fr. Cantalamessa.[3]

Among the acts of worship, another lip gesture is the kiss, when it expresses veneration for something or someone. Adoration is a special type of worship which involves a deep humbling of self "before the Infinite, and in devout recognition of His transcendent excellence."[4]

---

3. Cantalamessa, Fourth Lenten Homily.

4. William L. Sullivan, "Adoration," *Catholic Encyclopedia*, vol. 1 (New York: Robert Appleton, 1907), https://www.newadvent.org/cathen/01151a.htm.

The etymological meaning of the word adorer can be found in Latin languages: *ad orare*, from the Latin *os* (mouth), which properly means to bring to the mouth, to kiss. It's poignant to note that to adore is to stand humbly before a majesty that infinitely surpasses us, but which we can nonetheless approach, a God who allows himself to be encountered, whom we cannot only venerate but also love, and who can moreover become food for us. The kiss expresses the desire to be nourished by the other. To adore is to feed on God. We can put our hand over our mouth to send a kiss, but also to invite our lips to be silent. This is precisely what Job expresses at the end of his ordeal: *"Behold, I am of small account; what shall I answer thee? I lay my hand on my mouth"* (Jb 40:4).

Ultimately, the highest act of worship is silence. The closer we come to God, the rarer words are spoken, for we sense how powerless they are to express a mystery that only silence can truly honor.

Worship is a great good for man. If he humbles himself to it, acknowledges his lowliness, the effect on him is a glorified, exalted state: for, it is in worship that man realizes the most beautiful and profound capacities of his nature. Man finds a certain loftiness in acting and in transforming reality, but he finds a much higher glory in welcoming "something" that infinitely surpasses him, in admiring and contemplating an immense beauty that is offered to him. This is why he was created, and it is his greatest joy.

Eucharistic adoration

Eucharistic adoration is a place where prayer and worship often go hand in hand. It is a particular gift from the Lord for our ever-increasing need to be nourished and strengthened by his Eucharistic presence, especially in times of struggle and confusion. Of course, we need to be able to pray everywhere, to converse intimately with God in nature, while traveling, even in the midst of crowds. But Eucharistic adoration has gradually taken, and will increasingly take, a privileged place in the Church's piety.

Even if it can at times feel a little poor and dry, Eucharistic adoration is always a grace for the worshipper, a source of life for the whole Church, and a way of hastening the coming of the Kingdom for the whole world. When we are deprived of all personal satisfaction in prayer, we must be content to be like a candle, freely consumed in God's presence. Paradoxically, nothing is more fruitful than this accepted and offered poverty, before the God of glory who makes himself so poor for us.

11

Prayer and Liturgy

SR. CLAIRE OF THE REDEMPTOR GALLE

*Entering into contemplative prayer is like entering into the
Eucharistic liturgy: we "gather up" the heart, recollect our
whole being under the prompting of the Holy Spirit, abide
in the dwelling place of the Lord which we are, awaken
our faith in order to enter into the presence of him who
awaits us. We let our masks fall and turn our hearts back
to the Lord who loves us, so as to hand ourselves over to
him as an offering to be purified and transformed.*[1]

Prayer and the liturgy may sometimes seem like
distant or opposing realities: Prayer is a more personal dialogue and favors silence and an interior
life, whereas liturgy is communal, a public prayer of
the Church, that is lived according to a rite made up

---

1. *Catechism of the Catholic Church* (CCC), 2nd ed. (Rome: Libreria
Editrice Vaticana, 2000), no. 2711.

of gestures, words, and songs. Yet prayer and liturgy complement, serve, and call upon each other.

Dimension dialogue

Prayer and liturgy share the same dynamism and the same purpose: relationship and union with God. One more time, we remember the words of St. Teresa of Ávila who called prayer "nothing but friendly intercourse, and frequent solitary converse, with Him Who we know loves us."[2]

Meanwhile the liturgy, as the *Catechism of the Catholic Church* states, "is a meeting of God's children with their Father, in Christ and the Holy Spirit; this meeting takes the form of a dialogue, through actions and words.[3] In both prayer and liturgy, then, we find the dialogue that lies at the heart of Revelation.[4] This dialogue, evident in the one-on-one, heart-to-heart conversation of interior prayer, also constitutes the liturgy, which makes it visible through acclamation,

---

2. Teresa of Ávila, *Life*, p. 62.

3. CCC, no. 1153.

4. See Vatican Council II, Dogmatic Constitution on Divine Revelation *Dei Verbum* (November 18, 1965), no. 2, https://www.vatican.va /archive/hist_councils/ii_vatican_council/documents/vat-ii_ const_19651118_dei-verbum_en.html.

song, and prayer. In the liturgy, the faithful's voice is the privileged instrument of the believing heart that responds to God, like a bride to her Spouse, like a child to his Father. Joseph Ratzinger attests: "This structure of Word and response, which is essential to the liturgy, is modeled on the basic structure of the process of divine revelation, in which Word and response, the speech of God and the receptive hearing of the Bride, the Church, go together."[5] The future Pope Benedict XVI also explains that silence in the liturgy is necessary for this dialogue between God and man: "We respond, by singing and praying, to the God who addresses us, but the greater mystery, surpassing all words, summons us to silence."[6]

He reminds us that "we should expect the liturgy to give us a positive stillness that will restore us . . . For silence to be fruitful . . . it must not be just a pause in the action of the liturgy. No, it must be an integral part. . . ."[7] He continues, "[T]his silence is not just a period of waiting, something external. . . . Shared silence becomes shared prayer.[8]

---

5. Joseph Ratzinger, *The Spirit of the Liturgy* (San Francisco: Ignatius Press, 2020), p. 222.

6. Ratzinger, p. 223.

7. Ratzinger, p. 223.

8. Ratzinger, p. 225.

Liturgical silence is akin to the silence of prayer. It is made up of recollection, inner peace, attention to the essential, and inner dialogue with the Lord.

Liturgy: the source and end of all prayer

The liturgy, as participation in the prayer of Christ, addressed to the Father in the Holy Spirit, and as celebration of the mystery of Christ, is the source and end of all prayer.[9] This is what makes it a Christian prayer—Christ in all his mysteries is its center, leading us to the Father. The same Christocentrism is found in Carmelite prayer, so attentive to Christ's holy humanity as a path to transforming union with the thrice-holy God.

More concretely, the various elements of the liturgy, inspired by or drawn from the Word of God (readings, psalms, prayers, hymns, and so on), "reveal more deeply the meaning of the mystery being celebrated, assist in understanding the psalms, and prepare for silent prayer."[10] Similarly, "*lectio divina*, where the Word of God is so read and meditated that it becomes prayer, is thus rooted in the liturgical celebration."[11]

---

9. See CCC, nos. 1073 and 2655.

10. CCC, no. 1177.

11. CCC, no. 1177.

Living the liturgy with heart

Conversely, the quality of our prayer life, our *inner* prayer, influences the way we live the liturgy. It fosters harmony between the *external* dimension of the rite (proclamation of the Word of God, vocal prayers, singing, gestures) and our deepest heart: "The celebration of the Liturgy of the Hours demands . . . harmonizing the voice with the praying heart,"[12] and prayer serves this need.

Prayer thus fosters a liturgy that is worship in spirit and in truth, the place of encounter, of union with God, and of the sanctification of man. The *Catechism* states, "Prayer internalizes and assimilates the liturgy during and after its celebration."[13]

This is why prayer, recollection, and attention to God's presence before, during, and after the liturgical celebration allow him to bear all his fruit of grace in our lives.

Pray without ceasing

Just as time spent in prayer gradually imbues the whole of our existence with a spirit of prayer, time devoted

12. CCC, no.1176.
13. CCC, no. 2655.

to the Eucharist and the Liturgy of the Hours, also known as the Divine Office, can gradually transform our whole life into a liturgy, as the Cistercian Dom André Louf testifies.

> Any authentic liturgy [tends] to spread, to extend throughout the day, to invade every available space, in time, in place, and above all in the hearts of those who pray. Authentic liturgy always bears fruit beyond itself. It rubs off on life, tending to transform the whole of it into a ceaseless liturgy.[14]

What is said here about liturgy can also be said about prayer, so that authentic prayer always bears fruit beyond itself. It rubs off on life, and tends to transform the whole of it into ceaseless prayer. As the Second Vatican Council's Constitution on the Sacred Liturgy states: "The Divine Office, as the public prayer of the Church, is the source of piety and the nourishment of personal prayer."[15]

As we can see, prayer and liturgy are intrinsically linked and mutually nourishing.

---

14. André Louf, *L'œuvre de Dieu, un chemin de prière* (Éd. Lethielleux, 2005), p. 157.

15. Vatican Council II, Constitution on the Sacred Liturgy *Sacrosanctum Concilium* (December 4, 1963), no. 90. Vatican website: vatican.va.

A pithy tale

The following pithy tale is given to us by Dom André Louf to introduce his book on the liturgy as path of prayer. He writes that, at the time, "it was not only clerics who had some difficulty perceiving the link between liturgy and prayer."[16]

> In an ancient cathedral [. . .] is a venerable chapter of clerics busy reciting the Office. Suddenly, a violent storm breaks out. Lightning flashes and thunderclaps follow one another, drawing nearer. A shudder runs through the stalls, and the dean of the chapter, greatly moved, waves his hand and calls out to his confreres: "Let us stop the service, my brothers, to pray for a moment."[17]

As we consider the humorous moral, let us give thanks to God for the beauty of our call to seek him and to enter into his communion in all circumstances!

---

16. Louf, pp. 7–8.
17. Louf, pp. 7–8.

12

Prayer Life and the Cross

FR. JOËL MAISSONNI

The one who acts for the Kingdom does much. The one who prays for the Kingdom does more. The one who suffers for the Kingdom does everything.

FRANTISEK CARDINAL TOMASEK

The sign of the cross marks our entry into the Christian life through our Baptism and begins our liturgical, and often personal, prayers. But what is the relationship between the cross and our prayer life?

The *Catechism* defines the relationship very simply between the cross and the soul: "There is no other way of Christian prayer than Christ."[1]

Furthermore, our prayer reaches the Father through the prayer of Christ; "the prayer of Jesus involves a loving adherence to the will of the Father even to the Cross

---

1. CCC, no. 2664.

and an absolute confidence in being heard."[2] Through Christ's Cross, our prayer is no longer that of servants before their master, but that of children before their Father. Through the Cross of Christ, the Father accepts our prayers as the father in the parable embraces the prodigal son.

We might sometimes think, since we have been redeemed, since we are his sons and daughters, our prayer should no longer be directed towards the Cross, but towards the Resurrection! This is an illusion, for the Cross and the Resurrection are inseparable. At every Eucharist, we celebrate Christ's Passion and Resurrection.

Within our prayer, we too must take up his Cross and follow the prayer of Christ, who is the Way, in order to reach the Father's Heart (see Mt 16:24). It is in this participation of Christ's Cross that we make our prayer life fruitful. Our participation becomes action, for example, when we fast or keep vigil at night to support our prayer; or our participation is passive, when the Cross comes to touch our lives.

The Cross enriches our prayer

Our prayer ascends to the Father by the "elevator" of Christ's Cross; but, even more, our prayer finds all its

---

2. CCC, no. 2620.

fruitfulness when we live it "in" Christ's Cross. No matter the form of prayer, when the Cross "embraces" our flesh or our soul, Christ comes to pray in us, making our prayer fruitful. Let us consider some examples of siants before us living out different types of prayer through their suffering.

Prayer of petition

A dramatic example of petition in the Cross takes place on Calvary. The good thief unites his passion with that of Christ, and his seemingly senseless request on the threshold of his death is instantly answered: "Truly, I say to you, today you will be with me in Paradise." The other malefactor lives his passion in revolt, turned in on himself, and dies alone in his suffering (see Lk 23:39–43).

Prayer of intercession

Soon after St. Thérèse of Lisieux offered herself as a victim to Merciful Love in June of 1895, her body and soul were united to the Passion of Christ (April 1896). Seated at the table of sinners, she offered herself with Christ for them, and now spends her heaven doing good on earth, interceding for us with the Father.

Prayer of praise

An example of praise in the Cross is the praise of the three young men in the furnace (see Dn 3:23–25). Also consider that it was after St. Francis received the stigmata, when he bore the Passion of Christ in his flesh and was almost blind, that he wrote: "Be praised, my Lord."[3] Indeed, Christ told us himself, "Blessed are you when men revile you and persecute you and utter all kinds of evil against you falsely on my account. Rejoice and be glad, for your reward is great in heaven, for so men persecuted the prophets who were before you" (Mt 5:11–12).

Prayer of adoration

When the Cross "touches" our adoration, it's the moment when the vase breaks so that the perfume spreads and fills the whole house (see Mk 14:3–8; Jn 12:3).

At the foot of the Cross, St. John stands in pain and incomprehension before the mystery of the Passion, but he stands in adoration and contemplates the Heart of Christ forever open for us, that we may make

---

3. St. Francis of Assisi, *Canticle of Creation*, Catholic Online, www. catholic.org/prayers/prayer.php?p=3188.

our dwelling there. And Mary's Heart is opened by the sword so that all that her heart has guarded, pondered, and adored of the mystery of Christ may be delivered to those who stand with her at the foot of the Cross.

When St. Teresa of Calcutta hears Christ's *"I thirst!"* in the "I thirst!" of a poor man, the Cross invades her soul, and her adoration moves tirelessly from Christ on the Cross in the Blessed Sacrament to Christ on the Cross in the poor man.

For her in particular, the Cross is where prayer and the gift of self are but one.[4] Caring for the dying, she is a new Mary: *"In pouring this ointment on my body she has done it to prepare me for burial"* (Mt 26:12).

Reaching out to the poor of Calcutta, she lived out what the Community of the Beatitudes sings in a hymn dedicated to the holy Curé of Ars: "It is the Cross that carries you, not you who carry it." The Cross of Christ was what carried her to the poor.

Welcome the Cross

But when the Cross of Christ comes to touch us, do we welcome it in humble, trusting adoration, or do we harden our hearts to protect ourselves? If we welcome

---

4. See CCC, no. 2605.

it, we can begin to understand the words of St. Louis-Marie Grignion de Montfort: "No Cross, what a Cross!" For we welcome the fruitfulness—painful as all childbirth—that the Cross brings to our prayer and our adoration.

If we unite our small everyday crosses or the great trials of our lives with the Cross of Christ, then, to echo St. Paul, "*it is no longer I who pray, but Christ who prays in me*" (Gal 2:20). My prayer is, then, enveloped in the Heart of Christ, a Heart forever open in the heavenly Jerusalem since the Ascension, and my adoration participates in the eternal adoration that circulates within the Holy Trinity. But then, simultaneously, the Cross of Christ establishes me in the night: "*My God, my God, why hast thou forsaken me?*" (Mt 27:46). And like Christ in Gethsemane, like Thérèse of Lisieux or Mother Teresa, I don't know what to do: with no more than faith to move forward, loving abandonment to the Father's will, "*not as I will, but as thou wilt*" (Mt 26:39).

Is our dryness during times of adoration a sign of our participation in the Cross of Christ or linked to our tiredness, laziness, or lack of zeal? The answer is of course measured by the fruits. Our participation in the Cross infuses us with the fruits of humility, gentleness, goodness, peace, and profound joy, even in the midst of external storms.

May we not forget that every time the Church invokes God's blessing on our world, she accompanies her prayer with the sign of the Cross: "In the name of the Father, and of the Son, and of the Holy Spirit." Through the Cross, our prayer encounters God's blessing.

Spiritual exercise

At the start of mental prayer, let one of the seven words of Christ on the Cross inspire you and guide your prayer. After it, look for what this word has "opened" in your heart.

Mt 27:46: *"My God, my God, why hast thou forsaken me?"*

Lk 23:34: *"Father, forgive them; for they know not what they do."*

Lk 23:43: *"Today you will be with me in Paradise."*

Jn 19:26–27: *"Woman, behold, your son!* [. . .] *Behold, your mother!"*

Jn 19:28: *"I thirst."*

Jn 19:30: *"It is finished."*

Lk 23:46: *"Father, into thy hands I commit my spirit!"*

Job's testimony

Consider Job's testimony, found in chapter 42:13–15. Job shows us how the Cross transforms our prayer. Before the trial, God's blessing had granted Job seven sons and three daughters whose names we do not know. After the ordeal, the Lord again grants him seven unnamed sons and three daughters whom we are told were very beautiful, and whom Job gives a share of the inheritance with their brothers.

Why this sudden attention to his daughters? Through trial, his prayer of thanksgiving before God's blessing turns less towards efficiency (symbolized more, at least culturally, by the masculine) than towards fruitfulness (symbolized more by the feminine), less towards "doing" than towards "being," less towards action than towards contemplation. His Cross opened his heart to what was essential and transformed his prayer.

13

Aridity and its Causes

FR. JACQUES PHILIPPE

If we accept spiritual trials, it's not out of a desire to achieve perfection, which would involve a certain exaltation of the self. Rather, it is to submit to God's plan for the fulfillment of his will.[1]

MATTA EL MESKEEN

n the spiritual life, especially in prayer, we can experience moments of dryness. Prayer becomes heavy and boring, we don't feel much, our thoughts go in all directions without managing to settle down, time passes very slowly. The reasons for this aridity can be diverse.

---

1. Matta El Meskeen, *L'expérience de Dieu dans la vie de prière* (Éd. Abbaye de Bellefontaine, 2019), p. 285.

Spiritual laziness

A first possible cause of dryness is a certain spiritual laziness. Flowers in a garden that isn't watered enough inevitably wither. Are we paying enough attention to giving our soul what it needs to stay awake and fervent in God's desire? Spiritual laziness can take many forms. First, a lack of fidelity to prayer: the less we pray, the less we want to pray. Another form is a lack of vigilance in providing our soul the stimulation it needs: readings, retreats, nourishing teachings, spiritual guidance that forces us to take stock of our life on a regular basis, and regularity in receiving the sacraments, confession in particular.

A frequent cause of spiritual laziness is also the flight from the Cross: seeking too much comfort and ease in, human satisfactions, not accepting wholeheartedly the annoyances and difficulties of life, and refusing all the little sacrifices by which the soul is strengthened.

Another cause of laziness can be too much concern for affection for others or overemphasis on busyness—work, sports, social networking, or any hobby or practice, including the apostolate sometimes!—so that in the end there's not much room left in the heart for God.

Deeper causes often underlie laziness. One of these is the fear of complete surrender to God. We can have a very strong feeling that, if we start praying seriously, God will attack the state of mediocrity in which we have settled. What can also make us lazy is a certain discouragement: the feeling of not moving forward, of always having to deal with the same difficulties, of falling back into the same mistakes. To restore courage to the soul, we need to restore hope, an absolute confidence in God's mercy.

Psychological considerations

A second cause of dryness can be psychological. Excessive fatigue, tension, and stress can make prayer difficult or even impossible. St. John of the Cross speaks of "melancholy." In modern terms, we would speak of depression, burn-out, or other psychological situations in which one has no desire for anything; a kind of apathy. In such cases, the first thing to do is to remedy these human problems as far as possible, before tackling the issue on a spiritual level. It's all too easy to speak of a "spiritual night" in situations that have little to do with it.

Permission from God

The third possible cause of dryness is spiritual. Difficulties and poverty in the practice of prayer are an invitation to base our relationship with God no longer on the tastes, representations, and images we used to rely on, but rather on an act of faith. What we can feel or taste of God is not God. For a deeper contact with God, which only faith can give, it is necessary to go through a certain deprivation of sensible experiences and imaginative representations. These are not bad, but there is a risk of getting bogged down in them, whereas if we follow the path of simple, pure faith, we find ourselves on a much safer path.

To this God-given dryness, we simply have to consent. It's not comfortable, but it's an opportunity to exercise a stronger, purer faith, because it relies on God alone.

According to St. John of the Cross, this entry into dryness is often linked to an evolution in the prayer life, the passage from "meditation" to "contemplation." It's a question of gradually entering a form of prayer in which human activity is much reduced and simpler, more receptive than active. Prayer becomes simply a general, loving attention to God, with no particular emotions or representations to support it.

John of the Cross gives three criteria for recognizing this type of dryness, which must abide together. The first is that, whereas the soul used to find joy and pleasure in it, it now experiences a great difficulty and

reluctance to meditate, reflect, and pray when considering particular realities.

The second is that this difficulty in meditating stems
neither from the aforementioned laziness (because then
the person has a strong desire to occupy himself with a
thousand things other than God) nor from the forms of
psychological apathy we've been talking about.

The third criterion is that the person, despite the
poverty of their prayer, has no real desire to be interested in anything other than God (they retain a great
concern for God, a fear of not loving him enough) and
they begin to feel an inclination to remain still, silent,
with no particular activity other than a general, loving
attention of the heart towards God.

Some may have scruples about following this inclination, because it seems the person is doing nothing,
but he or she must move in this direction. Sensibility
may be arid, with thoughts wandering left and right,
but the heart is present in a simple, loving attitude
of attention to God. This is true prayer, an authentic act of faith and love, which gradually deepens and
becomes very fruitful.

Dryness is sometimes a problem that needs to be
remedied, but it can also be a great grace, the gateway
to contemplation—to a new way of looking at things; a
simpler, more receptive prayer in which God secretly

communicates himself to the soul and enriches it with great goods.

Living through dryness
from St. Thérèse of Lisieux

> Nothing near Jesus, dryness! . . . Sleep! . . . Since Jesus wants to sleep, why would I stop? I am only too happy that he is not embarrassed with me, he shows me that I am not a stranger by treating me like this, because I assure you that he does not charge any expense to keep me in conversation![2]

> Sometimes when my mind is in such great dryness that it is impossible for me to draw a thought from it to unite myself to the Good Lord, I very slowly recite an "Our Father" and then the angelic greeting; so these prayers delight me, they nourish my soul much more than if I had recited them hastily a hundred times . . .[3]

---

2. St. Thérèse of Lisieux to Mother Agnes of Jesus, January 6, 1889 (Letter 74), https://archives.carmeldelisieux.fr/en/correspondance/lt-74-a-soeur-agnes-de-jesus-6-janvier-1889/.

3. St. Thérèse of Lisieux, Manuscript C, p. 25, Archives of the Carmel of Lisieux, http://archives.carmeldelisieux.fr/en/archive/manuscript-c.

14

Spiritual Struggle and Prayer

PASCAL MAILLARD

The knowledge of God does not dwell in a body that loves comfort.[1]

ST. ISAAC THE SYRIAN

Having considered the periods of drought, we can't fail to mention the action of the Enemy, for whom the practice of prayer is a real threat: he will do everything in his power to prevent it, or at least to delay it. Some distractions are psychological in nature, while others are inspired by the Enemy; it's up to us to learn to discern and better deal with them.

---

1. St. Isaac the Syrian, *Mystic Treatises*, trans. A. J. Wensinck (Amsterdam: Royal Academy of Sciences, 1923), p. 56, Internet Archive, www.archive.org/details/IsaacOfNinevehMysticTreatises/page/n57/mode/2up.

"*For we are not contending against flesh and blood, but . . . against the spiritual hosts of wickedness in the heavenly places*" (Eph 6:12). Paul's exhortation warns us that the Christian life, of which prayer is the cutting edge, calls us to engage in genuine spiritual combat. We are not alone in this battle: God himself protects us with the armor of his love, and we receive from him the weapons to resist and win.

As we know, prayer is the best way to be united with God. The stakes are vital. Prayer is the place where the torrents of divine tenderness flow into us. The fruitfulness of our apostolate will largely depend on the quality of our prayer. Is it that simple? No, because there are many obstacles; the most common are external, the most subtle are internal.

Obstacles to overcome

Some obstacles manifest themselves externally. For example, at the appointed time of prayer, we may think there are better things to do than pray, like those very concrete things whose immediate effectiveness we can see. We may suddenly fall asleep, have to make a phone call or send an email that has instantly become indispensable and urgent, or meet someone who is going to take up a lot of our time, and so on. These obstacles, which arise at the very moment we are about to pray, often bear the mark of the spiritual warfare that can be stirred up by the evil one: to delay or deflect everything that is good to make us lose sight of the absolute urgency of prayer.

Once these initial obstacles have been unmasked and overcome, we can be attacked more insidiously, from the inside: while we're settled and collected, we'll allow ourselves to purr along reciting beautiful formulas without putting our heart into prayer. Other distractions may arise, such as thoughts about the perfect menu for the next day, an essential purchase, or the ideal way to solve a current problem!

The evil spirit inside us can suggest to our conscience that our prayer is useless and torment us with nagging memories of sins we've already confessed, locking us up in a guilt that is sure to cut us off from God's love.

Another classic is imaginary conversations. Here we find ourselves embroiled in endless discussions with one or another person who makes us angry, who makes us suffer, or even with people we love and with whom we project ourselves into an illusory situation. So many stray thoughts pull us out of the present moment—in that precise moment when God is at hand and giving of himself.

Temptation can also come through impure thoughts, or we put on mental magnifying glasses that distort situations so that everything becomes dramatic and we lose our peace, and with it the presence of God. The enemy makes us anticipate, through our imagination, a difficulty, a suffering, even a great misfortune that will never actually happen! All of this is done to worry us.

In prayer, the evil spirit can also try to infect our wounds, past or present, and cause us to experience all kinds of emotions. The good Spirit will encourage us to offer our wounds.

Weapons for victory

Our perfect model is, of course, Christ himself. He truly experienced all things as we do, with the exception of sin: "*For because he himself has suffered and been tempted, he is able to help those who are tempted*" (Heb 2:18). In particular, he was tempted in the desert and in Gethsemane. His weapons? The Word of God and surrender to the Father.

For us too, there's no shortage of weapons for victory: calling on the name of Jesus, Prayer of the Heart, the sign of the Cross made slowly and fervently, or prayer in tongues where the Holy Spirit himself intercedes within us. An act of faith in the manner of

Thérèse of Lisieux who said "I just sing what I want to believe"[2] will dissolve the temptation to doubt. Sometimes, a vocal prayer in which every word is emphasized can curb the suggestions of any accusing spirit.

The important thing is to know how to discern spirits: to recognize and understand the subtlety of God's action within us and to nourish it, rejecting that which does not come from him. Ignatian spirituality can help us a great deal in this respect; it is akin to the practice of guarding the heart, so dear to the East.

On the other hand, the Virgin Mary, our mother, received from God himself the mission of crushing the serpent's head (see Gn 3:15). Reciting the rosary with the heart is a powerful weapon practiced by the saints. So is invoking our guardian angel, who constantly sees the face of God.

Last but not least, let's never forget what St. Francis de Sales recommends: while we can use distractions in prayer to make them the subject of our prayer, we must not face temptations head-on, as they will then grow stronger and we'll be defeated. It's a question of "slipping" out of their reach, of going "under the wave," as St. Dorotheus of Gaza also puts it:

---

2. St. Thérèse of Lisieux, Manuscript C, p. 7.

If someone for some reason is swimming in the sea, if he knows the art of swimming, then when a wave comes against him he ducks under it until it passes, and thereby continues swimming without harm. If he tries to oppose the wave, it will toss him up and can carry him a long distance away. When he continues swimming and another wave comes against him, which he also tries to oppose, it likewise pushes and thrusts him away and he only becomes fatigued without any benefit. But if, as I have said, he should dive beneath the wave and stay under it, it passes over him without doing him any harm, and he can keeping swimming as long as he likes, and go about his business. It is the same with temptations.[3]

Victory is God's

God allows spiritual warfare only insofar as it can make us grow and unite us more closely to him.

All these weapons are necessary, but we must never forget that God remains the master of everything: "[T]he Lord saves not with sword and spear; for

---

3. St. Dorotheus of Gaza, *Instructions*, Instruction 13, Russian Orthodoxy website, https://pravoslavie.ru/60892.html.

the battle is the Lord's and he will give you into our hand" (1 Sam 17:47). He is always in control, even when all seems hopeless. Job was tempted only with God's permission, and the fruit was of immense blessings, a true rebirth for Job, just as prayer is for us.

15

Prayer in Times of Trial

SR. TIDOLA ABDOU

For me, prayer is a surge of the heart, it's a simple look toward Heaven, a cry of gratitude and love amidst trial as well as joy; finally it's something great, supernatural, which expands my soul and unites me to Jesus.[1]

ST. THÉRÈSE OF LISIEUX

ayal's[2] family members were some of the victims of the explosion in the port of Beirut on the fourth of August, 2020, which killed 240 people and injured some 5,000. A year later, the young woman, although committed to a life of prayer, spoke of her desolation at not praying fervently: "I can't manage to pray, or to think about God. Time goes by and

---

1. St. Thérèse of Lisieux, Manuscript C, p. 25.
2. This name is fictitious (Editor's note).

I'm still asking him, why has he abandoned us? Why doesn't he bring justice to the victims? Why doesn't he answer our prayers?"

In fact, we are heirs to a pattern of prayer that we assume is perfect: to gather in silence before God for a consistent period of time, during which we experience an outpouring of good feelings and we make good resolutions.

Anything outside this picture, we surmise, is not "prayer." In difficult times, we often give up praying altogether, or we believe we're not praying if we don't recite our prayers fervently.

Biblical times

Scripture teaches us, through the experience of biblical characters, that we can open ourselves to union with God—the goal of prayer—through simple and accessible means, especially in difficult moments.

Was not Abraham prayerful when he believed God's promise to bless him and give him offspring from Sarah's womb, despite his and Sarah's advanced age (see Gn 15:1–7)? Didn't he pray for Sodom and Gomorrah, entering into communion with God and with those he wanted to save from perdition (see Gn 18:16–33)? Interior prayer means surrendering ourselves into God's hands, remembering his Covenant, presenting him with our requests—to the point of even bargaining with him!—and hoping against hope for the fulfillment of his promises.

Didn't Moses pray when Amalek came to fight Israel at Rephidim (see Ex 17:8-9)? His raised hands ensured Israel's victory. Prayer means taking our place on the holy mountain, where our God awaits us, and listening to him so we can be led to victory.

Here's yet another example: Didn't David pray throughout his life as shepherd, husband, father, warrior, and king? The psalms show us a man of flesh and blood who loved, worked, sinned, waged war, and even killed, and who knew how to invoke the God of his life in all these circumstances. Prayer means abiding in God and turning to him in joy and in distress, in sin and in grace, in misfortune and in blessing.

Jesus is a faithful witness to the prayer that unites him to the Father. He retired alone or with his disciples to pray (see Lk 5:16; 6:12; 9:18 and Lk 11:1-13). His final prayer in the Garden of Gethsemane reveals that God never leaves his friends alone in the face of trials, including death (see Mt 26:36-46; Mk 14:32-42; Lk 22:39-46). Jesus knows he does not pray alone: the angels are there. The Father is there, even if he seems to have abandoned Jesus. The Comforter is there. Knowing this, Jesus can put himself in the Father's hands and carry out his will to the end. He knows that death will not have the last word.

Our times

Thérèse of Lisieux recounts two very instructive episodes on how she lived prayer. She writes:

> It seems to me when Jesus descends into my heart, that he is happy to find himself so well received and I am happy too . . . All this does not prevent distractions and sleep from coming to visit me, but on leaving the thanksgiving seeing that I have done it so badly, I resolve to spend the rest of the day in thanksgiving.[3]

Thérèse understood that she must not let herself be led by the spirit of fear, but that she must make the most of her miseries. When Jesus says to us, as he said to Peter: "*Simon, are you asleep? Could you not watch one hour?*" (Mk 14:37), and we offer him our sleep, promising to be more awake next time, this is a form of prayer, to hear and accept Jesus' words.

---

3. St. Thérèse of Lisieux, Manuscipt A, p. 80, Archives of the Carmel of Lisieux, archives.carmeldelisieux.fr/en/archive/manuscript-a/.

Thérèse recounts another episode in which she offered up an unbearable noise that distracted her during prayer time:

> I tried to unite myself with the good Lord, to forget the little noise . . . everything was useless. I felt the sweat which flooded me and I was obliged to simply make a prayer of suffering, but while suffering, I sought the means to do it not with annoyance, but with joy and peace, at least in the intimacy of the soul. So I tried to like the unpleasant little noise; instead of trying not to hear it (an impossible thing), I focused on listening to it well as if it had been a delightful concert, and all my prayer (which was not that of quietude) was spent offering this concert to Jesus.[4]

There is a story of a rabbi who was led to his death in the concentration camps, and who got through his ordeal by reciting the *Shema' Israel* (see Dt 6:4–9) aloud. Some laughed at him, saying, "Why do you keep praying and calling on your God? Where is he to save you?" The man replied, "I've always repeated this prayer, telling God that I love him with all my heart, soul, and strength, and now it's time to prove it. My God is with

---

4. St. Thérèse of Lisieux, Manuscript C, p. 30.

me." The rabbi's prayer was a cry of confidence in spite of the ordeal.

Whether it is a prayer of well-being or suffering, of praise or desire, the saints invite us to abandon our defenses, our views, and our ideas in order to embrace our life as it is, and offer it to Jesus so that he can offer it to the Father as he is. The saints tell us that the essential thing is our willingness to follow Jesus, to persevere in our desire to be his, and to unite ourselves to him, in body, soul, and spirit.

God is with us

On the one hand, we want to unite with God and help bring about the Kingdom through our religious practices and daily struggles, for *"the kingdom of heaven has suffered violence, and men of violence take it by force"* (Mt 11:12). On the other hand, the Lord invites us to rest in his Heart, in the face of life's harsh trials and endless crises. So, we pray by offering up our physical pain, by putting before God all the anger we feel at illness, or by weeping at our inability to forgive a betrayal. To pray with no other weapon other than faith, hope, and love, is the prayer that God, who scrutinizes hearts and minds, accepts (see Jer 11:20; 17:10 and 20:12; Ps 138:13–24).

Forever lasts a long time

The words of the author Père Jérôme in his book *Car toujours dure longtemps* speaks of fidelity to the Lord at all times.

> Let us consider the reproach of the Lord to those who pretend to be faithful: "Your love is like a morning cloud, like the dew that goes early away" (Hos 6:4).

> It is not difficult, in fact, to say "I love you." The difficulty begins when we say "forever," and especially when it comes to realizing it. After all, forever lasts a long time. As long as the attraction to the beloved remains strong, we remain attached to him or her without effort or trouble. For the attraction not to diminish as reality unfolds, the one who loves must be able to renew their love, to maintain it at least in its original state. For what yesterday rightly attracted you deserves to attract you again today if you have the strength to rise above fuss to fidelity, recrimination to rhythmic melody.[5]

---

5. Père Jérôme, *Car toujours dure longtemps* (Le Sarment-Fayard, 1986), pp. 162–163. Our translation.

16

Overcoming Acedia

SR. MARIE PIA ZURBACH

Despondency [says]: ". . . my opponents, by whom I am now bound, are psalmody and manual labour. My enemy is the thought of death. What completely mortifies me is prayer with firm hope of future blessings."[1]

ST. JOHN CLIMACUS

Acedia, also known as despondency, is a complex reality comprised of laziness, boredom, and discouragement. It is also a spiritual state of weariness, disgust with work and prayer, torpor, and craving for anything and everything.

All the Desert Fathers see it as one of the main obstacles to prayer. Still called the "midday demon," it is seen as the heaviest and most overwhelming of

---

1. John Climacus, trans. A. L. Moore, *The Ladder of Divine Ascent* (New York: Harper & Brothers, 1959), step 13, no. 16, p. 140.

passions. A trial and a temptation, it becomes a sin when we abandon ourselves to it, giving up all effort.

Signs

Bodily instability

The urge to move all the time, to change places. This instability reveals a deeper instability of the heart.

A vague and general dissatisfaction

A disgust for one's duty, finding everything bland, and no longer expecting anything.

Despondency leads one to flee from one's duties and to look for other activities or duties, in the belief that they will be more fulfilling. It causes negligence in ordinary duties and an inclination to do as little as possible.

The inner emptiness acedia generates can lead the person to undertake multiple activities and paths that are not necessary, without any real satisfaction. Hopelessness and depression can follow.

A darkening of the soul and spirit

A slackening of the soul in spiritual activities. Despondency seeks to draw one away from the regularity and constancy necessary for prayer, and to flee from silence with vain dialogue. Zeal for God seems to have disappeared.

Coptic Orthodox monk and theologian Fr. Matta El Meskeen notes:

> Man rises to pray and finds neither the words of prayer nor the strength to continue it. When he sits down to read, the book is in his hands, according to Isaac the Syrian, as if it were made of lead, and can remain open before his eyes for a whole day without his understanding a single line. The intellect is scattered, unable to concentrate and understand the meaning of words; the will that presides over all activity is dissolved.[2]

Its causes and reasons

Overwork can be the cause: indulgence in excessive activity, or asceticism beyond one's strength, which causes a breakdown. Or, out of scruples, a person multiplies their activities, doing more than required, and suddenly is unable to accomplish even the minimum, which once seemed so little.

Certain climates, hot and unhealthy, are seen by the Fathers as a cause of Despondency.

It is not without reason that God allows such a trial for the soul that seeks him. Fr. Matta El Meskeen discerns,

---

2. El Meskeen, p. 91.

God withdraws from the soul its ability to rise, so that it does not risk rising above its possibilities of balance and endurance, and consequently falling and crashing. It is then a safeguard of the soul's life, preserving it from spiritual pride.[3]

This trial rectifies an erroneous conception the soul may have of God. God does not love the soul because of her efforts or diligence: she is just as dear to him in moments of darkness and inability. God doesn't need the soul's fervor or works to love her: these must be a response to God's love for her, not the price to be paid for receiving that love.

Finally, the soul aims to strengthen faith in God beyond the sensible. Faith must "rise above abandonment and lead man to keep his trust in God, in his mercy and solicitude, despite all the tribulations he goes through."[4] A certain parallel can be drawn with the "nights of the soul" of St. John of the Cross.

Remedies

Crying

This first remedy recommended by the Desert Father Evagrius Ponticus is the act of sorrow, of recognizing

---

3. El Meskeen, p. 294.

4. El Meskeen, p. 300.

our helplessness, our need for a Savior, and trusting
that he will come to us.

Prayer and the Word of God

Offer a short prayer that we can still throw up to heaven
or a verse of Scripture that we can repeat as often as possible. The prayer handed down by John Cassian, "*Save
me, O God!*" (Ps 69:1) is as relevant as ever; meditating
on the end of days, bringing man face to face with his
destiny, can be a wake-up call.

Hold on at all costs, with patience

Don't get discouraged, do not abandon everything, but
hope against hope. Continue to do what you can, even
if it seems like very little.

Said one priest,

> As I found myself in this difficult ordeal. . . . I
> could not not say my Office of prayers because this
> demon [of despondency] wouldn't let me go. I was
> content to hail the Cross and prostrate before it. As I
> held on for a little moment, the demon was repelled
> by the power of the Cross.[5]

---

5. Joseph Hazzaya, *Lettre sur les trois étapes de la vie monastique*,
trans. Paul Harb and François Graffin (Turnhout, Belgium: Brepols,
1992), p. 35.

The necessary virtue here is patience. Isaac the Syrian had a similar experience:

> The compassionate Father, when he wants to deliver from their temptations those who are truly his children, does not take away their trials, but gives them the patience to bear them. It is in patience that they receive all good things, for the perfection of their souls.[6]

Relaxation

An outing, simple manual work, and improved physical hygiene will also help.

Fraternal charity

This is paramount and must be practiced in all its forms.

It's important not to let go of God's hand, to stay in relationship with him, remembering that "*the sufferings of this present time are not worth comparing with the glory that is to be revealed to us*" (Rom 8:18). When and as God wills, sooner or later, in this life or the next, we will experience total deliverance.

---

6. El Meskeen, p. 304.

17

Silence and Speech

FR. JOËL MAISSONNI

Everything that is great and creative is formed from silence.[1]

MAURICE ZUNDEL

In the beginning . . .

In the beginning was the Word: God said, and it was. His creative Word organized the original hustle and bustle, the Word which gives life. And the fruit of this Word of God is infinitely good. Through his Word, his love is expressed, takes shape, is given. The purpose of the Word is to establish us in this invigorating relationship of love.

---

1. Maurice Zundel, "The Blessed Sacrament," May 28–31, 1940, Maurice Zundel Foundation, posted June 2011, https://mauricezundel.com/26-28-06-2011-le-saint-sacrement/.

Human speech is an instrument of communion in love, yet it remains deeply wounded by original sin. The spoken word can become a lie, it can divide, condemn, destroy, kill.

On the other hand, silence can also be a place of communion in love: hand in hand with a sick or dying person, silence is often a communion and compassion stronger than any words. Two lovers, hand in hand, express their love more through silence than through words.

But these silences must be the fruit of a given word, and be a profound presence to the other. For our silences, too, bear the wound of sin. Silence can be unspoken indifference, contempt, isolation, anger, clenched fists. Silence can break communion (in a married couple, for example), just as it can break a relationship.

A necessary purification

Speech and silence, in our human relationships as in our spiritual life, need to be purified and supported by each other. Silence according to God is not the absence of speech; it is beyond speech. Good silence is first and foremost listening: listening to God so as to allow ourselves to be called, instructed, led, and loved by him.

Or listening to others to give them their full place. Or listening to our deepest heart in inner silence, so we can discern beyond our passions. It's not uncommon for us to speak—even with very fine words—at the cost of failing to listen to the other person.

Some people tend to flee from or break the silence out of fear of being alone with themselves. A good silence is also a sign of autonomy and respect for the other person or what he or she is going through. Others find it hard to speak up for fear of expressing themselves (exposing themselves) in front of others.

Listening and responding

If silence is listening, then it's even more important to listen to—to encounter—the other person rather than their words; to listen more with the heart than with the head.

After the proclamation of the Gospel in the Mass, the priest or deacon says: "The Gospel of the Lord," and we respond: "Praise to you Lord Jesus Christ." We praise the Lord first, as he comes to meet us in his Word. Only then do we meditate on and welcome the precise Word he gives us this day. It's a question of welcoming this Word not at the level of our reasoning—always ready to debate, to argue, and very often to defend ourselves—but with the heart; a heart which allows itself to be instructed and shaped by the Word in the image of the Virgin Mary who kept and pondered all these words and events in her heart (see Lk 2:51). Our listening, our silence, our words must become humble and chaste in the school of the Virgin Mary.

If silence is first and foremost listening, our words must first and foremost be responding. Not a "reaction" to the word of another, but a "response" in which our deepest heart invests itself.

Silence and prayer

Of course, it's in prayer that silence is both the most precious and the most difficult to experience. It's a good idea to begin the time of prayer with a glance at the Virgin Mary, to make ourselves receptive to God's visit. This is not a time for meditation, but for communion, hand in hand with the Lord.

Then, throughout the time of our prayer, the Prayer of the Heart (continual prayer, the Jesus Prayer) should help us to remain humbly in the presence of God at the deepest level of our hearts. During this time, our thoughts won't stop turning: our everyday concerns, a word or attitude that hurt us, old wounds or dreams surfacing, thoughts of discouragement, or sometimes even darker thoughts, such as jealousy or murmuring. Should we try to muzzle these thoughts, or run away from them? Is it not better to simply hand them over, let them flow into God's heart, without dwelling on them?

Among the Apostles, Simon Peter is often the first to speak, sometimes enlightened by the Spirit, sometimes getting in the way of God's plan (see Mt 16:13-23) and even when he doesn't know what to say (see Mk 9:6).

However, after his triple denial, when he meets the Lord's gaze, Peter says nothing, but weeps bitterly. In front of the empty tomb on Easter evening, when Christ manifests himself to the Apostles, Peter says nothing. A few days later on the shores of Lake Tiberias when John exclaimed to Peter, *"It is the Lord!"* (Jn 21:7), Peter didn't argue, but threw himself into the water. By the fire, he says nothing.

Jesus takes the initiative by questioning him. Then, at last, Peter can speak the only words Jesus was waiting for: *"Lord, you know everything; you know that I love you"* (Jn 21:17).

In Mary's school

Let us contemplate Mary and John by the Cross. There they stand, facing Christ, their hearts torn by what they see. They do not rebel. They do not intervene. They let God act for the salvation of the world, even if they cannot understand everything at that moment. They keep and meditate in the depths of their hearts what they contemplate.

Behind them they hear the cries of the crowd: the insults, the blasphemies, the cries of hatred express-ing all human despair and revolt. They hear, but they don't listen. They let it flow into the heart of God. Mary lets the sword of these words open her heart, and she lets it all flow into the heart of Christ, soon to be pierced. This is how we must stand before Christ in adoration, silently surrendering to him all that dwells within us and all the cries of the world. May we be like John, who saw Christ's heart opened by the spear, but then witnessed the empty tomb, and came to believe that God has held nothing against us and that his Salvation is victorious.

18

Interior Life

SR. MARIE PIA ZURBACH

How good is this presence of God within us, in this inti-
mate sanctuary of our souls. There, we always find Him
even though . . . we no longer feel his presence, but He is
there all the same, maybe closer still.[1]

ST. ELIZABETH OF THE TRINITY

"Behold, the Kingdom of God is in the midst of you" Jesus tells us (Lk 17:21), and St. Paul says, "We are the temple of the living God" (2 Cor 6:16).

God dwells in us and invites us to dwell in him. Our interior life is that place in the heart, that center of the soul, where he is present. The interior life is also our ability to dwell in that place, and to return to it quickly.

---

1. Elizabeth of the Trinity, Letter 47, in Joanne Mosley, *Elizabeth of the Trinity: The Unfolding of her Message, vol. 1, In Her World and in Community* (Oxford: Teresian Press, 2020), pp. 125–26.

St. Elizabeth of the Trinity will be our guide in this chapter, among others, as she writes: "Ah, I wish I could tell everyone what sources of strength, of peace and of happiness they would find if they would only consent to live in this intimacy."[2]

God dwells within us

St. John of the Cross marvels at God's presence in the souls who love him:

What joy for the soul to learn that God never abandons it, even in mortal sin; how much less in a state of grace!

What more can you desire, what more can you seek without, seeing that within you have your riches, your delight, your satisfaction, your fullness and your kingdom; that is, your Beloved, Whom you desire and seek? Rejoice, then, and be glad in Him with interior recollection, seeing that you have Him so near.[3]

"It is in 'this little heaven' that He has made in the center of our soul that we must seek Him and above

---

2. Letter 302, quoted in Conrad de Meester, OCD, introduction to Elizabeth of the Trinity, *Complete Works*, vol. 1, *I Have Found God*, trans. Aletheia Kane, OCD (Washington, DC: ICS Publications, 1984), p. 29.

3. John of the Cross, *Spiritual Canticle*, stanza 1, nos. 8–9, p. 21.

all where we must remain."[4] asserts Elizabeth. She continues,

> Pacify my soul; make it your heaven, your beloved abode and the place of your rest; may I never leave you there alone; but may I be there totally, totally awakened in my faith, all in adoration, totally surrendered to your creative action.[5]

But to remain in this "heaven," let us first listen to Jesus saying to us, as to Zacchaeus, *"Make haste and come down; for I must stay at your house today"* (Lk 19:5).

> "I must stay in your house!" It is my Master who expresses this desire! My master who wants to dwell in me with the Father and His Spirit of love, so that, in the words of the beloved disciple, I may have "communion" with Them.[6]

What then happens, once Zacchaeus, having descended from his sycamore tree, welcomed Jesus into his house? In an instant, Zacchaeus, the rich chief tax

---

4. Elizabeth of the Trinity, *Heaven in Faith*, no. 32, in *Complete Works*, vol. 1, p. 108.

5. Elizabeth of the Trinity, "Elevation to the Blessed Trinity," in Jean LaFrance, *Learning to Pray According to Sister Elizabeth of the Trinity*, trans. Florestine Audette, RJM (Sherbrooke, Quebec: Médiaspaul, 2003), p. 47.

6. Elizabeth of the Trinity, *Last Retreat*, no. 43, in *Complete Works*, vol. 1, pp. 161–16.

collector, became detached from the love of his riches and became capable of the magnificent gesture of sharing with the poor! What could have achieved such a result so quickly and joyfully? The evangelist does not tell us that Jesus asked him to share his possessions, but only that he asked to stay with him.

We too can hope, from this descent into our deepest heart where God resides, for a full and deep conversion. As Fr. Jacques Philippe says,

> Human beings are not purified from the outside inwards, but starting from within. Not so much by a moral effort we make, but by discovering a Presence within us and letting him act freely.[7]

Let us remain in God

Elizabeth writes:

> "Remain in Me." It is the Word of God who gives this order, expresses this wish. Remain in Me, not for a few moments, a few hours which must pass away, but *"remain . . ."* permanently, habitually. Remain in Me, pray in Me, adore in Me, love in Me, suffer in Me, work and act in Me.[8]

---

7. Jacques Philippe, *Thirsting for Prayer* (New York: Scepter, 2014), p. 62.

8. Elizabeth of the Trinity, *Heaven in Faith*, no. 3, pp. 94–95.

By seeking to dwell in our hearts where God is present, we reach out to the very source of life, who has the power to renew all things. Dwelling in our hearts is to have our roots in him, receiving strength, light, advice, and grace for our interior and exterior life. More and more, we will act according to him, and no longer according to knee-jerk reactions or our own woundedness.

In addition to the time we devote solely to prayer, here are a few attitudes that will help us to move in this direction:

- Become accustomed to returning often and quickly to our hearts where God is present
- Favor a listening attitude
- Give up our own ideas and wills when we have to
- Seek detachment in general
- Love interior silence and contemplation which can be present even during external noise and action

Mary, our role model

Let's look at Mary, living in the presence of God, who *"kept all these things, pondering them in her heart"* (Lk 2:19).

It seems to me that the attitude of the Virgin during the months that elapsed between the Annunciation and the Nativity is the model for interior souls, those whom God has chosen to live within, in the depths of the bottomless abyss. In what peace, in what recollections Mary lent herself to everything she did! How even the most trivial things were divinized by her! For through it all the Virgin remained the adorer of the gift of God! This did not prevent her from spending herself outwardly when it was a matter of charity: the Gospel tells us that Mary went in haste to mountains of Judea to visit her cousin Elizabeth.[9]

The powerful praise of the Magnificat flowed from Mary's deep interior life; Elizabeth of the Trinity perceived in her own interior life that she would always be "the praise of glory" of the Holy Trinity. May they both help us to inhabit and deepen our own interior lives!

Spiritual exercise

During the day, identify short moments when you can return to God's presence within: while turning on the computer, while waiting for the bus or at the checkout, or while walking around the house. Through the name of Jesus or a familiar invocation, descend into your heart.

---

9. Elizabeth of the Trinity, *Heaven in Faith*, no. 40, pp. 110–111.

19

Daily Prayer

GUILLEM FARRE

*For it is not so much of our time and so much of our atten-
tion that God demands; it is not even all our time and all
our attention: it is ourselves. For each of us the Baptist's
words are true: "He must increase and I decrease." . . .
Let us make up our minds to it; there will be nothing "of
our own" left over to live on.*[1]

C. S. LEWIS

Keeping in touch

"Go in the peace of Christ," says the celebrant when the
Mass is over . . . and we can understand in those words
the meaning: "Live now, in your daily life, what you have
received." After any time of prayer—adoration, the Divine
Office, Mass, or Scripture, for example—comes the

---

1. C. S. Lewis, *How to Pray: Reflections and Essays* (San Francisco:
Harper One, 2018), p. 68.

moment when we leave the sacred in order to reemerge into the earthly reality, into everyday life and worries. How do we keep in touch with God?

Aware of the separation between the secular world and the sacred, Christianity brought about revolutionary unity of these two dimensions. The sacred penetrates the secular through the Incarnation of Christ: God eats, God gets dirty, God walks and moves, God works, and so on. What good news! God is present in our daily lives. So we can keep in touch with him in all circumstances. We need to be reminded of this truth because human beings tend to separate, to classify, to keep a certain distance from God. This echoes the fundamental fear recounted in the Book of Genesis: *"I was afraid . . . and I hid myself"* (Gn 3:10).

Our God is the God of encounter and communion. He is the one who comes to take us where we are. In a homily delivered in Genoa on May 27, 2017, Pope Francis affirmed, "We pray in order to take everything to God, to entrust the world to him. Prayer is intercession. It is not tranquility; it is charity. It is asking, seeking, knocking" (see Mt 7:7).[2] Some spiritual paths run the risk of making an erroneous distinction

---

2. Pope Francis, Homily for Eucharistic Concelebration, Genoa, Italy, May 27, 2017. Vatican website: vatican.va.

between the sacred and the profane, reducing prayer to a search for psychological tranquility or inner harmony, cut off from life. The Pope reminds us that we pray to bring everything to God.

This is the key to keeping in touch with God at the heart of our activities: life itself. For life is the milieu in which our prayer and our contact with him arise and are nourished. The one who prays is not the one who is cut off from the world, but the one who knows how to live the real, the present, at every moment, and find in it the mysterious and hidden—but so very real—presence of God.

Pope Francis says that to reawaken passion for the Kingdom is to announce it and bring it to the most needy. We are asked to "develop a spiritual taste for being close to people's lives and to discover that this is itself a source of greater joy."[3]

Everyday life, with its worries, its difficulties, its activities, and also its worldly joys, is the place where this discovery of a spiritual taste, of a higher joy, is made possible. This experience sheds new light on Jesus' command to watch and pray at all times (see Lk 21:36). St. Paul also recommends, *"Pray at*

---

3. Francis, Apostolic Exhortation *Evangelii Gaudium* (November 24, 2013), no. 268. Vatican website: www.vatican.va.

all times in the Spirit, with all prayer and supplication"
(Eph 6:18).

Keep the fire burning

How can we keep in touch with God? We must, essentially, relearn how to live our daily lives. Two attitudes help us in this conversion: cultivating a spirit of wonder and seeking meaning in everything.

Cultivating a spirit of wonder

Christian philosopher Francesc Torralba says that "surprise is the beginning of questioning and the foundation of the development of knowledge in all its facets."[4] This necessarily requires questioning the meaning and origin of things and astonishment at the fact of existence. This capacity for wonder makes a spiritual life possible and opens the door for us to enter the Kingdom. It is the secret of little children: *"Truly, I say to you, unless you turn and become like children, you will never enter the kingdom of heaven"* (Mt 18:3).

---

4. Francesc Torralba, *Inteligencia espiritual* (Barcelona: Plataforma Editorial, 2011), pp. 116-117.

Searching for meaning

The other attitude that keeps us in touch with God is to seek meaning in all we do. The Jewish psychologist Viktor Frankl once said that the "will to meaning" is a fundamental desire: to give meaning to life, to have a meaningful existence, to find a reason, a motivation.[5]

Torralba emphasizes that the meaning of life encompasses at least three dimensions: the meaning of the multiple events that make up our existence (this presupposes that life, with its ups and downs, has a logic); the direction of our life (this presupposes the possibility of fulfillment); and the link between the value of life and joy.[6]

We can ask ourselves: In the multitude of things I do throughout the day, what is the meaning of each of these commitments? Why am I doing all this? Do I recognize a call from God? Do I see a mission in my daily life?

These questions can also help us make choices about the activities we carry out. If we let ourselves be led by existence without finding meaning in it, then our lives are empty, and we must urgently pray to the

---

5. See Viktor E. Frankl, *The Will to Meaning: Foundations and Applications to Logotherapy* (New York: Plume, 2014).

6. See Torralba, pp. 116–117.

Holy Spirit, "Come, Holy Spirit, come! And from your celestial home shed a ray of light divine! Come, Father of the poor! Come, source of all our store! Come, within our bosoms shine."[7]

By working on these attitudes, we'll be able to keep an inner fire, the kind that grace kindles in sacred moments of encounter with the Lord. In a logic of communion and unity, the sacred sphere and the secular sphere are not opposed, but nourish each other. Our lives are sources of spirituality and prayer. At the same time, prayer helps us to live our daily lives in God. In this way, all the means that help us to unite ourselves more closely to Christ, to be more docile to the Holy Spirit, will help us to make life itself the place where we meet the Lord and others.

Let us go in the peace of Christ!

---

7. Sequence, Readings for Pentecost Sunday, May 19, 2024, United States Conference of Catholic Bishops, https://bible.usccb.org/bible/readings/051924-Day.cfm.